RESTORATIVE READINGS

RESTORATIVE READINGS

THE OLD TESTAMENT, ETHICS, AND HUMAN DIGNITY

EDITED BY

L. Juliana Claassens

AND

Bruce C. Birch

FOREWORD BY

Walter Brueggemann

PICKWICK *Publications* · Eugene, Oregon

RESTORATIVE READINGS
The Old Testament, Ethics, and Human Dignity

Pickwick Publications
An Imprint of Wipf and Stock Publishers
199 W. 8th Ave., Suite 3
Eugene, OR 97401

www.wipfandstock.com

ISBN 13: 978-1-62564-721-4

Cataloguing-in-Publication Data

Restorative readings : the Old Testament, ethics, and human dignity / edited by L. Juliana Claassens and Bruce C. Birch, with a foreword by Walter Brueggemann

xxvi + 156 p. ; 23 cm. Includes bibliographical references.

ISBN 13: 978-1-62564-721-4

1. Ethics in the Bible. 2. Violence—Biblical teaching. 3. Strangers—Biblical teaching. 4. Immigrants—Biblical teaching. 5. Human rights. 3. I. Claassens, L. Juliana M., 1972–. II. Birch, Bruce C. III. Brueggemann, Walter. IV. Title.

BS680.E84 B575 2015

Manufactured in the U.S.A.   05/12/2015

In Memory of
Prof Russel Botman, Rector and Vice-chancellor,
Stellenbosch University, South Africa
October 18, 1953–June 27, 2014

Whose vision that "the *child* of the *farm owner* and the *child* of the *farm worker* should have an equal opportunity to become a Matie" continues to inspire us to work for a more just and humane world.

Contents

Contributors

CHERYL B. ANDERSON is Professor of the Old Testament at Garrett-Evangelical Theological Seminary in Evanston, Illinois. She joined the faculty there after completing her doctoral work at Vanderbilt University in 2000. Prof. Anderson is also an ordained elder in the United Methodist Church (Baltimore-Washington Conference). She is the author of *Women, Ideology, and Violence: Critical Theory and the Construction of Gender in the Book of the Covenant and the Deuteronomic Law* (T. & T. Clark, 2004). Her newer book, *Ancient Laws and Contemporary Controversies: The Need for Inclusive Biblical Interpretation*, was published by Oxford University Press in 2009. Her current research interests involve contextual and liberationist readings of Scripture in the age of HIV and AIDS. Email: cheryl.anderson@garrett.edu.

BRUCE C. BIRCH studied at Perkins School of Theology, SMU (MDiv) and Yale University (PhD). He taught at Iowa Wesleyan College and Erskine College before coming to Wesley Theological Seminary where he taught Hebrew Bible for thirty-eight years and served twelve years as Dean. He is currently Dean Emeritus and Professor Emeritus of Biblical Theology at Wesley Theological Seminary, Washington, DC. His works include *Let Justice Roll Down: Old Testament, Ethics, and Christian Life* (Westminster John Knox); "1 and 2 Samuel"; *The New Interpreter's Bible*, Vol. 2 (Abingdon); *Bible and Ethics in the Christian Life* (with Larry Rasmussen, Augsburg); *A Theological Introduction to the Old Testament* (with W. Brueggemann, T. Fretheim, and D. Petersen, Abingdon); and twelve additional books. He served as translator for 1 and 2 Samuel for the Common English Bible. Email: bbirch@wesleyseminary.edu .

NTOZAKHE SIMON CEZULA studied at Stellenbosch University, South Africa (BTh, MDiv, LicTheol, PhD). After serving as pastor in the Uniting Reformed Church in Southern Africa, he currently is Lecturer of Old Testament in the Faculty of Theology, Stellenbosch University, South Africa, with a research focus on a Theology of Reconstruction in the biblical traditions as well as in the (South) African context. Email: cezulans@sun.ac.za.

L. JULIANA M. CLAASSENS studied in South Africa and the USA (PhD, Princeton Theological Seminary) and taught at St. Norbert College, Green Bay, WI, Baptist Theological Seminary Richmond, VA, and Wesley Theological Seminary, Washington, DC. She currently is Professor of Old Testament with a research focus on human dignity in the Faculty of Theology, Stellenbosch University, South Africa. Her works include *The God who Provides: Biblical Images of Divine Nourishment* (Abingdon, 2004), and the most recent, *Mourner, Mother, Midwife: Reimaging God's Liberating Presence in the Old Testament* (Westminster John Knox, 2012). Email: jclaassens@sun.ac.za.

DION A. FORSTER has a PhD in Systematic Theology (SA) and is currently completing a second PhD at Radboud University, Holland. He was formerly the Dean of John Wesley College, the seminary of the Methodist Church of Southern Africa. Dion is a senior researcher in the Beyers Naudé centre for Public Theology and a Senior Lecturer in Systematic Theology and Ethics, with a focus on Public Theology, at Stellenbosch University, South Africa. His most recent book is entitled *Between Capital and Cathedral: Essays on Church and State Relationships* (University of South Africa Press, 2013). Email: dionforster@sun.ac.za.

JACQUELINE E. LAPSLEY is Associate Professor of Old Testament at Princeton Theological Seminary (Ph.D., Emory University). She coedited, with Carol Newsom and Sharon Ringe, *A Women's Bible Commentary*, 3rd ed. (Westminster John Knox Press, 2012), was associate editor of *A Dictionary of Scripture and Ethics* (Baker Academic, *2011*), and authored *Whispering the Word: Hearing Women's Voices in Old Testament* (Westminster John Knox Press, 2005). She serves on the editorial boards of *The Catholic Biblical Quarterly* and *Hebrew Bible and Ancient Israel*. Email: jacqueline.lapsley@ptsem.edu.

DOUGLAS LAWRIE is an Associate Professor in the Department of Religion and Theology of the University of Western Cape, South Africa. Some of his major publications include a textbook on biblical hermeneutics (edited with Louis Jonker, *Fishing for Jonah (anew)*, Stellenbosch SUN Press, 2005) as well as a book on biblical rhetoric, *Speaking to Good Effect: An Introduction to the Theory and Practice of Rhetoric* (Stellenbosch SUN Press, 2005). Email: dlawrie@uwc.ac.za.

ESIAS E. MEYER studied in South Africa (DTh, Stellenbosch), Oxford, and Marburg and was a minister in the Dutch Reformed Congregation of Strand North in Strand, Western Cape. He is currently a Senior Lecturer in Old Testament Studies in the Faculty of Theology, University of Pretoria, South Africa. His works include *The Jubilee in Leviticus 25: A Theological-ethical Interpretation for a South African Perspective* (Lit Verlag, 2005). Email: sias. meyer@up.ac.za

CHARLENE VAN DER WALT is currently serving as the Gender, Health, and Theology Master's Program Coordinator at the Department of Old and New Testament, Faculty of Theology, Stellenbosch University, South Africa. She also works as a researcher for Inclusive and Affirming Ministries (IAM) on a part-time basis and is an ordained Minister of Religion, serving as pastor to a congregation in Maitland, South Africa. Her book, *Toward a Communal Reading of 2 Samuel 13:Power and Ideology within the Intercultural Bible Reading Process* has recently been published (Intercultural Biblical Hermeneutics Series 2; Elkhart, IN: AMBS, 2014). Email: charlenevanderwalt@sun.ac.za.

GERALD WEST teaches Old Testament/Hebrew Bible and African Biblical Hermeneutics in the School of Religion, Philosophy, and Classics in the University of KwaZulu-Natal, South Africa. He also works extensively with the Ujamaa Centre for Community Development and Research, a project in which socially engaged biblical scholars and ordinary African readers of the Bible from poor, working-class, and marginalized communities collaborate for social transformation. Among his publications are: edited with H. de Wit, *African and European Readers of the Bible in Dialogue: In Quest of a Shared Meaning* (Leiden Brill, 2008); editor of *Reading Other-Wise: Socially Engaged Biblical Scholars Reading with Their Local Communities* (*Semeia Studies* 62, Atlanta/Leiden: SBL and Brill, 2007); *The Academy of the Poor: Towards a Dialogical Reading of the Bible* (Pietermaritzburg: Cluster, 2003); and edited with Musa W. Dube *The Bible in Africa: Transactions, Trajectories and Trends* (Leiden: Brill, 2000). He is general editor of the *Semeia Studies* series and the *Journal of Theology for Southern Africa*. Email: West@ukzn.ac.za.

Foreword

IT HAS NOT BEEN an easy time for the Bible as of late. As the so-called Biblical Theology Movement ebbed away and more acute and self-knowing social science criticism of the Bible has emerged, interpreters have begun to notice with great specificity the dark and hard parts of the text, most particularly the pervasive violence in the textual tradition. Thus we have an explosion of new titles on the theme. As scholars have noticed this, so the broader reading public has noted the same, surely because of the chaos into which our world seems to be freely falling. It has been a scramble in the last generation of interpreters to find credible ways to acknowledge and come to terms with the violence that contradicts both our conventional reading of the Bible as an ethical resource, and our own ethical horizons that have been compromised in complex ways. The critique of ideology at work in both text and interpretation, or more precisely the alliance of truth with power (Foucault) has turned out to be a way to proceed, a way vigorously utilized in this volume. Any innocence about the Bible or about our own societies is long since passed, even though we may sometimes wish for a modicum of innocence on both fronts.

Any attempt to consider the Bible as a resource or guide for ethical reflection, as this volume seeks to do, of necessity must begin with the awareness that there can be no direct move from text to contemporary practice; for that matter, no "application" of the Bible. That of course is not a new insight. Already Luther had insisted that for people of faith, trust is not in the Bible but in the gospel for which the "Bible" is only a frail carrier. But we still have the work of disabusing many who want and seek to take the biblical text for direct application. That of course is a temptation for those conservatives who want to preserve the status quo of social arrangements; they can readily find texts to support exclusionary practices. But it is also a temptation of some theological liberals who operate with a very small "canon within the canon."

Of course, for the writers of these fine essays there is a hermeneutical key that operates, even if it is not frontally articulated. It is that human dignity is indispensable for all persons, and eventually appropriate dignity for all non-human creatures as well; this is the test of truthfulness. Perhaps the best account of that hermeneutical key is offered by Terry Eagleton in which he argues that the biblical affirmation of the "scum of the earth" is the deepest claim for truth, the claim of serious gospel faith, and the answer to the so-called "new atheists."[1] The essays in this volume do not speak of the "scum of the earth," but they do attend to the vulnerable and powerless, and most especially to immigrants, those without legal standing. There is no better measure of the truthfulness of the Bible or the measure of responsible, faithful ethics than attentiveness to the vulnerable. Because the Bible does so in some of its trajectories, it is important not to dismiss the Bible wholesale as some critics are prepared to do.

It is important to do the harder task of adjudicating the text, of exposing ideology where it operates, to recognize texts that urge exclusion and diminishment of some for the sake of protecting the interests of others, all in the name of truth. Derek Flood, in his book, *Disarming Scripture*, has recently considered the way in which the Bible itself is an exercise in quoting older texts, but quoting them with perceptive editing in order to overcome and correct with freedom, to drop out of texts those elements that offend against human dignity or sensibility.[2] Such "editing" and "correction" constitute, he shows, a biblical principle of freedom in interpretation that is commensurate with an ethical practice of freedom for human dignity. Such a process, he shows, is not "cherry picking" as Bill Maher has recently suggested; nor is it supersessionism of a programmatic kind that wants to scuttle what is old. It is rather the way in which the process of traditioning works. Because every formulation of tradition is context-specific and reflects values and passions of a moment, the only responsible way of continuing the tradition is to do such critical work and then in a freely imaginative way to engage in post-critical retrieval.

I love the idea expressed here that even Nelson Mandela was short of complete faithfulness to a vision of human dignity of an inclusive and consistent kind. But that he failed in the full implementation is simply to

---

1. Eagleton, *Reason, Faith, and Revolution*.
2. Flood, *Disarming Scripture* (forthcoming).

recognize that every step along the process of the tradition is incomplete. The important positive recognition is that there is a "Third Mandela," namely the people. The "people as Mandela" do not possess all of the critical tools we might prefer. But the "people as Mandela" have a keen sense about *vested interest voiced as ideology* (the partial claim for some presented as the proper claim for all) and about *bodily pain* that is imposed by the covert operation of vested interest. It requires no book learning to recognize both the ideology and the resultant pain.

It is likely not unimportant that this book features especially voices of interpretation from South Africa and the United States. No doubt this has come about because of the friendship and colleagueship of the two editors, Claassens and Birch. Beyond that happenstance, however, it is telling indeed that both of our societies are deeply funded by and inured to the practice of violence. Both societies have a long legacy of violence that grows out of class and a racial history in which the dominant class and race has preferred reading the narrative texts without any self-criticism. It turns out that such reading is violent, to go along with uncriticized violent social practices. Indeed a society is not likely to sustain violent social practices unless it is accompanied by a legitimating violent reading of normative texts. Wayne Booth has suggested a while ago that irony is a contemporary form of "smashing idols," that is, of exposing "imposed truth" to demolition. Interpretation in this volume is a way of diminishing the claims of texts and the claims of interpretation that are made too easily in the service of social arrangements that are thereby "kicked upstairs" as "givens" and no longer constructs. The practice of irony, so well done here, is to bring those "givens" back to the status of constructs that are open to transformation. As irony is applied to biblical texts, so irony is readily applied as well to contemporary societal claims, notably the claims of national exceptionalism and entitlement in the United States, and perhaps shared claims of entrenched privilege in both of our societies.

The practice of looking to the Bible for ethical guidance is undoubtedly important, but it must be done, as here, with deep self-awareness and self-criticism. Long ago Walter Harrelson suggested that there is an especially important linkage between the Decalogue of Sinai and the Helsinki Declaration of Human Rights.[3] Harrelson made that connection at a time when we were all more innocent than we are now. But his judgment on the matter is a good word to suggest that after all the degradation of human

3. Harrelson, *The Ten Commandments and Human Rights*, 173–201.

dignity in the biblical text, properly noted here, there is another trajectory of covenantalism without which we cannot do.

The editors and writers of this volume are to be thanked for continuing the hard work of contestation and adjudication done with honesty, clarity, and discipline. It is only such discerning work that may save us from readings that are too easy and domesticated. The Bible has always been occupied with contesting voices. It is both our reading habits and our socioeconomic status that are called into the dock by such interpretive work. We are, by this volume, invited back to the urgent work of contestation that is indispensable for our future. Such work makes certain that our "assured results" in both reading and in social relationships are way-stations along the way of an ongoing process of faithful living.

Walter Brueggemann,

Columbia Theological Seminary,
October 23, 2014.

BIBLIOGRAPHY

Eagleton, Terry. *Reason, Faith, and Revolution: Reflections on the God Debate*. New Haven: Yale University Press, 2009.

Flood, Derek. *Disarming Scripture*. (forthcoming).

Harrelson, Walter. *The Ten Commandments and Human Rights*. Overtures to Biblical Theology. Philadelphia: Fortress Press, 1980.

Acknowledgments

WE ARE GREATLY APPRECIATIVE for the Hope Funding of Stellenbosch University that not only made it possible for Bruce Birch to come to Stellenbosch but also brought together some of the best of South African Old Testament scholars on the theme of the Old Testament, Ethics, and Human Dignity. Thank you also to Estelle Muller and Helette van der Westhuizen for all their work before and during this stimulating conference.

We want to thank Pickwick Publications for offering a home to *Restorative Readings*. It has been a pleasure working with you. A sincere word of gratitude goes to Ria Smit who has done a marvelous job copy-editing the manuscript into the correct format.

Also to our U.S. colleagues, Jacqueline Lapsley and Cheryl Anderson, as well as to our new colleague in Systematic Theology and Ethics at Stellenbosch University, Dion Forster: We appreciate that you took the time to read and comment on our book. Your voices are evidence that the conversation goes on.

And finally to Walter Brueggemann who was willing to write the foreword to this book—your example of seeking to read the Old Testament in our complex contemporary context(s) continues to inspire.

Introduction

L. Juliana Claassens,
Faculty of Theology, Stellenbosch University

THE BIBLE IS A dangerous book. This statement always raises quite a bit of reaction among first year theological students. And at first, some express disbelief and even anger: The Bible? The Word of God? Dangerous?

An example from South Africa's apartheid history, though, serves to illustrate this point. In his essay, "The Dangers of Deuteronomy," Ferdinand Deist shows how a gross translation error in the first Afrikaans translation of the Bible (1933) was used to provide proof of God's "intent" to keep races separate. So Deut 23:2(3 MT) prohibits the offspring of an incestuous relationship (NRSV "illicit union," Hebrew *mamzēr*) to become part of the congregation of God (*qahal yahweh*).[1] The Afrikaans translation, *"baster"* ("a child born from parents of different races"), shows a sharp divergence from the original meaning, and most likely found its inspiration in the similar form of the old Dutch translation, "bastard," which incidentally also altered the meaning of the original word to mean "a child born out of wedlock." For ordinary people in the pews who had little access to Hebrew, these biblical words were taken at face value as signifying that no person of

---

1. This verse most likely should be read together with the next verse, according to which "no Ammonite or Moabite [even to the tenth generation] shall be admitted to the assembly of the LORD" (Deut 23:3(4 MT))—a verse that refers back to Genesis 18, according to which the Ammonites and Moabites are said to be born out of the illicit union between Lot and his two daughters.

color should be part of God's church, which together with a general under-standing of apartheid theology (that propagated different races to be kept separate based on a divinely ordained creation order), contributed to the formation and preservation of apartheid in South African churches and society.[2]

Deist goes on to show in his article how a beleaguered Afrikaner community in an apartheid South Africa identified with Israel in the book of Deuteronomy who were equally threatened at the time and, as a result, drew strong divisions between "us" and "them"—in the case of the *ḥerem* in Deut 7:1–2 even imagining the other to be completely annihilated. For instance, Deuteronomy's explicit prohibition against Israel mixing with the indigenous people (e.g., Deut 7:3–4), as well as the laws forbidding mixing different entities such as plowing an ox and donkey together (Deut 22:10), or wearing clothes made of a mixture of linen and wool (Deut 22:11), pro-vided the scriptural support for the South African immorality act prohibit-ing mixed marriages.[3]

Further examples of the troubling legacy of the Old Testament are well documented by a recent book by Eric Seibert, *The Violence of Scripture: Overcoming the Old Testament's Troubling Legacy*. Seibert introduces his book by telling a chilling story of New England settlers drawing on the vio-lent massacre in Judges 20 in order to justify the killing of seven hundred elderly men, women, and children of a Pequot village—the officer second in command that day writing that "sometimes the Scriptures declareth women and children must perish with their parents. Sometimes the case alters; but we will not dispute it now. We have sufficient light from the Word of God for our proceedings."[4] Add to this the Bible's role in encouraging violence against women, justifying slavery, and perpetuating hate crimes against gays and lesbians, and one may wonder why anyone would still want to read this book that has caused so much harm.

And yet, something in this book compels readers to keep on reading and indeed to overcome the violent legacy of particularly the Old Testa-ment. Several recent treatments have offered readers excellent hermeneuti-cal tools for mitigating the possible harmful effects of the Bible. For instance,

2. Deist, "The Dangers of Deuteronomy," 26–27.

3. Cf., e.g., the revealing comment by the theologian and poet, J. D. du Toit (Totius): "We may not unite what God has divided. The council of God is realized in pluriformity . . . Consequently we do not want any equalization or bastardization." Quoted in Deist, "The Dangers of Deuteronomy," 23.

4. Cited in Seibert, *The Violence of Scripture*, 1–2.

Eric Seibert offers his readers, in a very accessible and thought-provoking manner, a way of reading the Old Testament nonviolently, among others by "developing good reading habits" and by becoming "ethically responsible readers," as the title of one of his chapters suggests.[5] And in his book, *The Immoral Bible,* Eryl Davies outlines and evaluates various approaches that have been used to deal with the troubling legacy of the Old Testament, including the Cultural Relativists' Approach, the Canonical Approach, the Paradigmatic Approach, and finally the Reader-Response Approach.[6]

These approaches share a commitment that our biblical interpretations should be informed by an ethics of accountability, something that was articulated compellingly by the SBL president, Elisabeth Schüssler Fiorenza, during her 1987 Presidential address. She argues as follow:

> If scriptural texts have served not only noble causes but also to legitimate war, to nurture anti-Judaism and misogynism, to justify the exploitation of slavery, and to promote colonial dehumanization, then biblical scholarship must take the responsibility not only to interpret biblical texts in their historical contexts but also to evaluate the construction of their historical worlds and symbolic universes in terms of a religious scale of values.[7]

We have come a long way since Schüssler Fiorenza's course-setting words. Feminist, postcolonial, and queer interpretation have all offered us tools for engaging in biblical interpretations that are truly ethical in nature, and over the years have put forth numerous readings of biblical texts that deconstruct harmful interpretations and reconstruct interpretations that are life-giving in nature.

A helpful image that captures this ethical nature of the interpretative task shared by many of these approaches comes from Jacques Derrida, who builds on the work of the Jewish philosopher Emmanuel Levinas. Derrida describes the text that is handed down to us as a woven cloth, and the reading process as a creative process that involves the following two actions. In the first instance, reading implies for Derrida a "cut" into the cloth, suggesting the language Levinas and Derrida often use to describe

---

5. Ibid., 61–94. In subsequent chapters, Seibert suggests means of "Confronting [the] Canaanite Genocide and its Toxic Afterlife" (95–114) as well resisting the use of the Old Testament in order to justify war (115–28), and finally also strategies for preventing violence against women (129–46).

6. Davies, *The Immoral Bible,* 44–138.

7. Schüssler Fiorenza, "The Ethics of Biblical Interpretation," 15.

the interpretative process, i.e., "rupturing" or "interrupting." Part of the reading process is to "unmake the cloth," to rupture or tear open what has been handed down to the reader. However, a second important action in the interpretative process has to do with the restoration of the cloth which, according to Derrida, can be described in terms of the beautiful image of embroidering, or one could say "mending." In reading, the interpreter is to take up some hidden thread and strengthen or accentuate it by embroidering upon it, hence creating a richly textured fabric. The image of embroidering is particularly appropriate as it communicates the point that the reader is not pulling a thread out of thin air, but that the reader is following that which is already present in the text.[8]

A further important point regards the question of what is responsible for these acts of tearing and mending that form an integral part of ethically inclined biblical interpretation. Levinas would argue that this interruption comes from the outside, when the "said" (his term for the natural tendency of discourse to become fixed or frozen over time) is interrupted by the encounter with "the other."[9] As he powerfully states:

> In proximity the absolute other, the stranger whom I have "neither conceived nor given birth to," I already have on my arms, already bear according to the biblical formula, "in my breast as the nurse bears the nursling." He [sic][10] has no other place, is not autochthonous, is uprooted, without a country, not an inhabitant, exposed to the cold and heat of seasons. To be reduced to having recourse to me is the homelessness or strangeness of the neighbor. It is incumbent on me.[11]

Even though Levinas refers very much to the flesh and blood others with whom we share the world (we do not have to look too far to really see the face of the other: the homeless, the hungry, the poor, the sufferers of HIV/AIDS, the victims of war, racism, and sexism), it is important to note

---

8. For a good description of Derrida's use of Levinas in this regard, cf. Gibbs, *Why Ethics?*, 86–113. Cf. also Levinas, *Otherwise than Being or Beyond Essence*, 170–71; Derrida, "At this Very Moment in this Work Here I Am," 26–28.

9. Levinas, *Otherwise than Being*, 88–89.

10. Tamara Cohn Eskenazi relates here something of the feminist critique of Levinas when she asks the following pointed question: "How is it, for example, that Levinas can be so eloquent about the importance of facing 'the widow, the orphan, and the stranger,' yet always speak of the stranger as 'he'?", "Love Your Neighbor as an Other," 145.

11. Levinas, *Otherwise than Being*, 91.

that these voices of the other that may be responsible for new insight and transformation also show up within the text.[12]

Such a reading would imply that one identifies with the other in the text, with the "Hagars" in the narrative world. Tamara Eskenazi argues that by means of stories like that of Hagar, who functions in the text as "the paradigmatic 'Other' (cf. the pun of the name: Hagar/ger/stranger) . . . the reader is compelled to sympathize with the other, the one who is not 'us': the woman, the slave, the one from the 'other side of the tracks,' other group, other 'religion,' other class."[13] Similarly, Jione Havea notes that this love for the Other implies the

> courage to *alter*-read for lost figures, and for disfigures, in such places as the stories of the non-Israelite firstborns not passed over at Egypt, of the exodus generation who died in the wandering, of the "dwellers of the land" lurked (Num 13) and displaced in Joshua-Judges, of Ezra-Nehemiah's "people of the land," and in the cries in/of the stories of the Cains and Abels of history.[14]

This volume, with the title *Restorative Readings*, very much shares this desire to read ethically as outlined above. It reflects the efforts of seven South African scholars joined by seasoned scholars in the field of Bible and Ethics, namely, Bruce Birch, Cheryl Anderson, and Jacqueline Lapsley, who all engage in biblical interpretation that can rightly be described as restorative readings. The interpretations of selected Old Testament texts included in this volume all exhibit some aspects of Derrida's twofold task of tearing and mending the texts that have been handed down to us, inspired by the real and imagined "other(s)" in the text and our world at large.

Restorative Readings is the result of a very interesting conference held in 2013 at the Faculty of Theology of Stellenbosch University and made possible by the University's Hope Project. The Hope Project was the brainchild of our former rector, Russel Botman, who quite unexpectedly passed away while we were in the final stages of wrapping up this project (June 28, 2014). Prof Russel Botman, a theologian himself, was of the opinion that universities should not only be places of teaching and learning where the production of knowledge occurs, but that universities should also be engaged in society, actively seeking to make a difference in the world. Prof Botman, to whose life and vision this volume is dedicated, challenged us

12. Gibbs, *Why Ethics?*, 90; Jacques Derrida, *Margins of Philosophy*, 134–35.

13. Eskenazi, "Love Your Neighbor," 148.

14. Jione Havea, "To Love Cain More Than God," 111–12.

to not shy away from the world's most pressing problems but to use the best of our (interdisciplinary) research to protect and restore people's human dignity. The contributions to this book are hence grouped together around three such tough problems that plague South Africa today, but also the United States and communities around the rest of the world: Violence, Injustice, Xenophobia.

Restorative Readings is framed by a contribution by Bruce Birch who, ever since he wrote the important book, *The Bible and Ethics in the Christian Life*, together with Larry L. Rasmussen, has been deeply committed to contemplating the ways in which the Bible's restorative potential might be unlocked. Concluding responses come from Cheryl Anderson[15] and Jacqueline Lapsley,[16] who both over the years have distinguished themselves as ethically engaged biblical interpreters. And the last word comes from a new colleague of us at the Faculty of Theology of Stellenbosch University, Dion Forster, a systematic theologian and ethicist, who shares with my co-editor Bruce Birch as well as respondent Cheryl Anderson the distinction of being Methodist.

Our hope is that this volume of essays that reflects our respective journeys of engaging in restorative readings of the Old Testament may contribute to the larger vision of the promotion of human dignity that manifests itself in the call to resist violence, injustice, and xenophobia that on a daily basis threaten the well-being of individuals and groups in different parts of the world.

L. Juliana Claassens

Stellenbosch,
July 17, 2014

15. Cheryl B. Anderson, *Women, Ideology, and Violence*; Anderson, *Ancient Laws and Contemporary Controversies*.

16. Jacqueline E. Lapsley, *Whispering the Word*; M. Daniel Carroll R. and Jacqueline E. Lapsley, *Character Ethics and the Old Testament*.

BIBLIOGRAPHY

Anderson, Cheryl B. *Ancient Laws and Contemporary Controversies: The Need for Inclusive Biblical Interpretation*. Oxford: Oxford University Press, 2009.

———. *Women, Ideology, and Violence: Critical Theory and the Construction of Gender in the Book of the Covenant and the Deuteronomic Law*. 2nd ed. London: Bloomsbury, 2005.

Birch, Bruce C., and Larry L. Rasmussen. *Bible and Ethics in the Christian Life*. Rev. ed. Minneapolis: Augsburg, 1989.

Carroll, M. Daniel R., and Jacqueline E. Lapsley. *Character Ethics and the Old Testament: Moral Dimensions of Scripture*. Louisville, KY: Westminster John Knox, 2007.

Davies, Eryl W. *The Immoral Bible: Approaches to Biblical Ethics*. London: T. & T. Clark, 2010.

Deist, Ferdinand. "The Dangers of Deuteronomy: A Page from the Reception History of the Book." In *Studies in Deuteronomy: In Honour of C. J. Labuschagne on the Occasion of His 65th Birthday*, edited by Florentino García Martínez, 13–29. Leiden: Brill, 1994.

Derrida, Jacques. "At this Very Moment in this Work Here I Am." In *Re-Reading Levinas*, edited by Robert Bernasconi and Simon Critchley, 11–50. Bloomington, IN: Indiana University Press, 1991.

———. *Margins of Philosophy*. Chicago: University of Chicago Press, 1985.

Eskenazi, Tamara Cohn. "Love Your Neighbor as an Other: Reflections on Levinas's Ethics and the Hebrew Bible." In *Levinas and Biblical Studies*, edited by Tamara Cohn Eskenazi, Gary A. Philips, and David Jobling, 145–57. Semeia Studies 43. Atlanta: Society of Biblical Literature, 2003.

Gibbs, Robert. *Why Ethics? Signs of Responsibilities*. Princeton, NJ: Princeton University Press, 2000.

Havea, Jione. "To Love Cain More Than God." In *Levinas and Biblical Studies*, edited by Tamara Cohn Eskenazi, Gary A. Philips, and David Jobling, 91–112. Semeia Studies 43. Atlanta: Society of Biblical Literature, 2003.

Lapsley, Jacqueline E. *Whispering the Word: Hearing Women's Stories in the Old Testament*. Louisville, KY: Westminster John Knox, 2005.

Levinas, Emmanuel. *Otherwise than Being or Beyond Essence*. Translated by Alphonso Lingis. Pittsburgh, PA: Duquesne University Press, 1998.

Schüssler Fiorenza, Elisabeth. "The Ethics of Biblical Interpretation: Decentering Biblical Scholarship." *JBL* 107/1 (1988) 3–17.

Seibert, Eric. *The Violence of Scripture: Overcoming the Old Testament's Troubling Legacy*. Minneapolis: Fortress, 2012.

PART 1

Old Testament, Ethics, Human Dignity: Framing the Question

1

The Moral Trajectory of the Old Testament Drama:

Creation, Exodus, Exile

Bruce C. Birch,
Wesley Theological Seminary

INTRODUCTION

THE THEME FOR THE "Restorative Readings Conference" held in September 2013 at Stellenbosch University, South Africa, which offered the impetus for this book, brings together three categories: Old Testament, Ethics, and Human Dignity. That juxtaposition itself begins to bring focus to our conversation. Ethics connotes critical reflection on the moral dimensions of human experience. Such reflection encompasses both the character and the conduct of individuals or communities. Related to the Old Testament, interest in ethics may focus on discovering, understanding, and critically assessing the morality of ancient Israel. This enterprise would seek to discover the *world behind the text*. But the ethics of this ancient world can never be fully recovered or systematically described. We catch glimpses of the moral world behind the text, and can gain enriched understanding of particular moments and social contexts, but such glimpses reflect different moments and voices in a rich and diverse story that does not reflect any unified system of morality for ancient Israel that can be recovered.[1]

The texts of the Old Testament have been passed on to us by processes in the ancient Israelite community that made judgments on witnesses that should be preserved and passed on to future generations. Another way of understanding the relationship of ethics to the Old Testament is to explore the *world of the text created by the formation of canon.* Although individual books may be studied for their moral witness (and at times diverse voices within single books), the formation of the canon sets up a larger conversation. There is a moral dialogue created by the existence of the canon itself that includes convergences, tensions, juxtapositions, continuities, and contradictions as ongoing generations receive the authoritative collection of witnesses, and engages those witnesses in light of the claim that these *texts are Scripture handed on from generation to generation.*

The introduction of a third category, i.e., a focus on "human dignity," makes clear that our concern is not simply with the morality of ancient Israel nor even the canonical witness as an end in itself. Human dignity is introduced as a moral category central to modern ethical challenges and placed as a social mandate in key documents such as the South African Bill of Rights and the United Nations Declaration of Universal Human Rights. We come together because, as Christians, we want to discover in our own Scripture the resources and the challenges that affect our engagement with the moral struggle for human dignity in today's world.

When we bring a particular arena of moral concern, such as human dignity, to the Old Testament the tendency is to seek guidance for moral conduct. In other words, we ask the question, "What shall we do?" Can we turn to the Old Testament as moral agents seeking guidance for ethical decisions, actions, and strategies that will promote and enhance human dignity in our contexts?

A significant segment of recent work on Old Testament ethics argues that we cannot. In a widely admired work, Eckart Otto[2] has concentrated on legal and wisdom texts as the only literature in the Old Testament focused

---

1. See especially J. Barton, "Understanding Old Testament Ethics." This entire paper also necessarily reflects categories and understandings developed in my previous work on Old Testament ethics. Representative of this work are my work in "Ethics in the OT" and *Let Justice Roll Down.*

2. Eckart Otto, *Theologische Ethik des Alten Testaments.*

on explicit moral norms.[3] He defends his focus on explicit moral texts as a protection from the collapse of Old Testament ethics into Old Testament theology or history of Israelite religion. But he further argues that these explicit moral texts are so closely tied to ancient social contexts in Israel that no "application" of insights from Old Testament ethics on any direct line to ethical concerns today should be attempted.

It is certainly true that the Old Testament, even in explicit legal or wisdom guidance, cannot be used as a simple manual to make moral decisions for us as modern people of faith. But how Israel made such decisions, and the values and principles undergirding such decisions, can be meaningful for our reflection on the Old Testament as a resource for our own moral formation.

I want to argue, however, that our definition of ethics is often too narrow to allow us to fully claim the resources of the Old Testament for the moral life of God's people today. Christian ethics is not simply concerned with moral conduct but also with moral character. Here the operative question is "Who shall we be?" The focus is not on moral decisions but on moral decision makers, individuals, and communities. I propose that we are shaped as God's people by the entire canon of Scripture handed on to us. We are shaped by the biblical story and its many different types of literature. We are shaped by witnesses in the text to Israel's encounter and relationship with God and to stories of success and failure in living faithfully within that relationship.[4]

As important as the legal and wisdom traditions are to Old Testament ethics, the explicit moral guidance they give does not exhaust the moral resources of the Hebrew canon. Far larger portions of the Old Testament are taken up by narrative and prophetic traditions, and these unfold a dramatic biblical drama where the moral relationship of God and Israel are shaped in relationship that begins with creation itself. Narrative accounts and prophetic proclamation reveals dimensions of a moral vision that continues to shape the community of faith from Israel through many generations to our own life as the people of God today.

Given that the entire Old Testament canon is seen as a shaping moral influence on those who claim its story as their own, one could hardly attend

---

3. Otto's judgment limiting the focus of Old Testament ethics only to legal and wisdom texts has been vigorously criticized, e.g. Barton, *Understanding Old Testament Ethics*.

4. This is the basic argument of Birch and Rasmussen, *Bible and Ethics in the Christian Life*, revised and expanded edition.

to its entirety in a single essay. For the purpose of this essay I will sample this story and its power to shape our moral life at three crucial points: creation, exodus, and exile. We cannot engage in close exegetical treatment, but will instead point to some of the elements in these witnesses that can shape us as moral agents concerned for human dignity.

CREATION

It is significant that the Hebrew canon opens with witnesses to God as creator of all things. The God we encounter in the opening chapters of Genesis is not Israel's God alone. The creator God in these chapters is *universal* in scope. Before the Old Testament begins to tell the story of God's relationship to a particular people in promise and covenant it is important to encounter God as creator in relationship to all persons and all things. This universality of God's relationship to all creation provides a framework for all of Israel's story as a particular people of God. To begin the biblical story with God as creator of all is a reminder that God cannot be claimed as identified with any segment of humanity over another.

At the end of each day in Genesis 1 God declares the *goodness of creation*, and in v. 31 God declares the entire creation to be "very good." As I have argued elsewhere,

> It was not everywhere evident in the ancient Near East that the created world was good. In other ancient religious traditions the world was filled with hostile and potentially dangerous powers. . . . The Hebrew creation testimony . . . proclaims that God has created the world as benevolent. The Hebrew word טוֹב is capable of indicating both moral and aesthetic qualities. On the one hand, it indicates the creation as beautiful, pleasing. It is something God takes delight in, and therefore is to be regarded with delight by us—not regarded with suspicion or fear. On the other hand, there is a moral dimension. As good, the creation is declared to be in harmony with the divine intention. . . . The affirmation of creation as good stands over against all efforts to consider the material world or our own full humanity as inherently evil, or as spiritually debilitating.[5]

The Yahwist creation narrative of Gen 2:4b–25 makes clear that in the Hebrew concept *all of creation is related.* אָדָם is not self-sufficient. A

---

5. Birch, *Let Justice Roll Down*, 81.

garden is provided for food and beauty (2:9). God declares that "It is not good that the אָדָם should be alone" (v. 18). God first creates animals and then, out of the human's own flesh, a companion (עֵזֶר). The introduction of man and woman implies social existence in all of its possibilities and re-sponsibilities. What is significant for ethics in the Old Testament is that the gift of relationship also brings responsibility. The human must care for the garden, must name and take responsibility for animals, and live in mutual community with other humans. The constant interaction with God implies a divine/human relationship as well. Thus, as moral agents we are never free to act only in self-interest since we are created with inherent intercon-nectedness to each other and the creation itself.

We have already begun to touch on the role of our own *humanity in creation*. The witness of the two creation narratives in Genesis is in sharp contrast to many other traditions in the ancient Near East. In the Babylo-nian creation story human beings are created from the blood of the traitor-ous god Kingu, who allied himself with Tia'mat, the embodiment of chaos. Thus, humans come into being as the product of guilt and punishment, and they are assigned to be the slaves of the gods by doing the work of the world and relieving the gods of such labor.[6] The testimony of Genesis 1–2 could hardly be a greater contrast. In 1:26, humans are created in the image of God. Far from slaves, humans are bearers in their own being of testimony to the Creator, and as those who reflect the sovereignty of God they are given dominion over the earth. Such dominion is conditioned by the gift of imaging God and not the granting of an inherent human right. This fits well with the relational themes of Gen 2:4b–25 where humans are also given the gift of free will (Gen 2:16–17). They are given the ability to make genuine moral choices, but also given the responsibility to live with the consequences of those choices. This represents the full reality of rela-tionship to God. God takes the risk of a relationship that allows genuine freedom and is willing to be the first victim of a broken relationship when the man and the woman choose disobedience (Genesis 3).

What follows goes beyond our creation theme, but the unfolding episodes of the primeval history shows the persistence of God to maintain relationship with humanity in spite of sinful choices and the consequent brokenness. Even God has a moment of regret over creation (Gen 6:6), but the righteousness of Noah allows for the reassertion of God's grace in the

---

6. See also Birch, "Ethics in the OT," 345.

face of moral degeneration.[7] This allows those who claim these biblical witnesses the gift of moral agency and the trust that even sinful choices will not exhaust our relationship with God, and it is in God that new beginnings are possible.

A special word must be said about the boldness of the assertion in Genesis that both male and female participate fully in the image of God and the commission to dominion as God's agents in creation (Gen 1:27). In Gen 2:21–24 man and woman are the result of the dividing of one flesh, the human creature, אָדָם. And in their one flesh they introduce the possibility of human community, created as עֵזֶר to partner with and help one another. The ancient world was a patriarchal world, but the Hebrew conception of creation saw a co-equal possibility for which we are created that makes gender subordination always a sign of broken creation (Gen 3:16).

How could these creation testimonies not be relevant to the moral character of the communities that claim them as Scripture, read them, and take them to heart? Our created humanity is characterized by dignity, relatedness, freedom, and responsibility. To settle for anything less is morally unacceptable and an evidence of broken creation. It is the nature of our biblical story that even in the face of broken creation God is not willing to accept that it cannot be restored. In effect, our moral life matters to God because sinful choices break relationship with the divine as well as the human community. In the next section, we will move to another part of the Old Testament story where the depth of God's commitment to stay in relationship reveals new aspects of God's moral character and our own—the story of the exodus.

EXODUS

The narrative traditions of the Pentateuch, historical books, and the stories scattered in the prophets and the writings are not primarily for entertainment, information, or reporting. These narrative traditions have shaped the identity of the ancient Israelite community, and that community understood its identity to be shaped in encounter with God. By handing these narratives on to succeeding generations through the canon it is clear that others are invited to claim these stories as defining of their own character and conduct as God's people.[8]

7. Birch, "Creation and the Moral Development of God in Genesis 1–11," 12–22.

8. While a good deal of work has been done on the role of narrative texts in NT ethics

Narrative traditions find their ethical function first by approximating the moral complexities of human experience. We do not exercise our role as moral agents in the neat frameworks of separate commandments or proverbs but in overlapping claims and values in social contexts. Narratives approximate the messiness of human life yet show models of central characters and communities making their way, not without mistakes and repercussions, but nevertheless living out a moral vision that has dignity and integrity. But a second and central dimension of the moral claim of these narratives is that the complexity of ethics in the midst of life is not negotiated alone but in relationship to a God who is engaged in the process of historical experience with Israel and with all subsequent generations who claim these stories as Scripture.

As an example of the moral richness of Old Testament narrative I will focus on the centrally important exodus story in Exodus 1–15 and the reverberations of this story through much of the canon. It is this story that constitutes the birth story of Israel as the people of God, and in it significant moral claims are made about the character of God and of those God calls into relationship. Once again we cannot treat these materials in close exegetical detail. We will lift up ethically important themes that are grounded in this central narrative of deliverance out of bondage in Egypt.

Israel's birth story begins in grinding oppression and slavery that nearly extinguishes any human hope of an alternative. "But they would not listen to Moses, because of their broken spirit and their cruel slavery" (Exod 6:9). The oppressive and genocidal policies of the Pharaoh leave little room for human hope, but this is a story of the power of God as capable of confronting the power of earthly empire. The unfolding story of the book of Exodus suggests that the condition of human suffering is not morally acceptable to God.

The story of Moses' encounter with God at the burning bush is first important as a story of the self-revelation of God. Exodus 3:7–8a is an important text for understanding the nature of God both theologically and ethically. In four verbal phrases dimensions of God's character are revealed that we have not fully seen thus far in the Torah. First, God says, "I have seen . . . and I have heard." But the divine regard has been particularly focused by the "misery of my people" and "their outcry on account of their

---

there have only been a few scholars focusing on the moral importance of OT narrative. See Birch, "Old Testament Narrative and Moral Address," 75–91, and Wenham, *Story as Torah.*

taskmasters." Divine caring is mobilized by human suffering. The Hebrew verb זָעַק is an outcry of pain and complaint, but it is not addressed to God; it is not prayer. God's regard is captured by the cry of the suffering and not by the need to observe religious ritual of any kind.

In the third verbal phrase God says to Moses, "I know their sufferings." The Hebrew verb "to know" (יָדַע) is not limited to cognitive knowing. It indicates an experiencing and entering into that which is known. It establishes ongoing relationship. God has chosen to become vulnerable by sharing human suffering.[9] This is an early biblical expression of a theme that, for Christians, reaches its fullest expression in the cross.

This leads to the final verbal expression in this text, "I have come down to deliver them." The moral character of God as one who cares for and shares human suffering now finds expression in the moral action of deliverance. God will open a way into the future for this people. God chooses to become engaged in human history in order to make a difference on the side of deliverance of those who are oppressed or marginalized. This is, of course, a major theme throughout the canon, Old and New Testament.

Although the Exodus story is centrally focused on the moral character and initiative of God there are several other important moral dimensions to the story. We will point to these but do not have space to fully develop them.

First, God's deliverance does not operate in isolation from human agency. The self-revelation of God at the burning bush is also the call of Moses. God chooses to engage human leaders alongside the divine activity and sometimes as the conduit of divine activity. Human moral concern cannot passively wait for the activity of God, but is called to be fully engaged in God's moral concern and moral action.

Second, the verbs of Exod 3:7–8b allow us to observe that moral norms in the Old Testament do not wait for the giving of commandment and law on Mt. Sinai. Moral norms in the Old Testament sometimes arise out of *imitatio Dei*, the imitation of God.[10] In seeing suffering, hearing cries of pain, making the pain of others our own, and taking action to create life-giving alternatives, God has already modeled the life of the community who would be God's people. Throughout the canon God demonstrates the

9. See Fretheim, *The Suffering of God*, for a groundbreaking study of this theme of divine vulnerability throughout the Old Testament.

10. A number of scholars have called attention to the importance of *imitatio dei* in Old Testament ethics. Barton, "Understanding Old Testament Ethics," 60–61; Hanson, *The People Called*, 30, 44.

qualities of character and the integrity of actions that should mark the community of faith. "For I am the LORD who brought you up out of the land of Egypt, to be your God, therefore you shall be holy, for I am holy" (Lev 11:45).

Third, God's salvation in Exodus does not focus on saving Israel from sin but is experienced as liberation from the oppression of a tyrant. Exodus 5–12 details a confrontation between Israel's God Yahweh and the Pharaoh of Egypt, the epitome of human earthly power. Thus, the Exodus story is a major corrective to an overly spiritualized conception of God's salvation. It is a confrontation of political power with divine power and at the same time a confrontation between the creative power of Yahweh and the forces of chaos (perhaps represented by the gods of Egypt). God's power is capable of moving toward wholeness regardless of earthly or cosmic power.[11]

Finally, the climactic crossing through the sea to new life in Exodus 14–15 becomes a paradigmatic event representing God's unexpected deliverance in the midst of distress that animates hope throughout the canon and into succeeding generations who read this story as Scripture. In terms of ethics it means that for those who trust in God's delivering power and grace situations marked by despair, grief and death can never have the final word because God's power always makes a further word of life and hope possible. In God's delivering grace there is always a way into the future.[12]

EXILE

The prophetic literature of the Old Testament contains a minimum of narrative and mostly consists of prophetic proclamation. However, the prophetic message only makes full sense when placed in the social context of Israel's story as detailed in the narratives of the historical books. In the past, the prophetic books have received attention for their ethical significance almost as if they could be abstracted from their Old Testament context as the source of timeless moral truths discerned by individuals of unusual moral insight.

The prophets stood within the theological and ethical traditions of the Israel that came before them. They knew and referenced the narrative traditions of Israel's story. They knew the covenant traditions of Israel's

---

11. The work of Terence Fretheim has especially emphasized the importance of creation theology throughout the Exodus story of deliverance, *Exodus*.

12. See Birch et al., *A Theological Introduction to the Old Testament*, 115–20.

relationship as God's covenant people and spoke of God's judgment and redemption in the context of that covenant understanding. Israel was held morally accountable by them for failure to exhibit the character and conduct expected of God's people. But they also understood themselves as called by God to proclaim God's word in the context of their own times and places and were bold to speak the word of the LORD in the first person, "Thus says the LORD."

To illustrate a particular moment of prophetic proclamation and its ethical implications I will focus on the preaching of the anonymous prophet we call Deutero-Isaiah whose message to Babylonian exiles is found in Isaiah 40–55. I choose this prophet because the disregard of covenant moral mandates for justice, righteousness, compassion, and steadfast love, especially by Judah's leaders, have brought disaster upon Judah and Jerusalem in 587 BCE in the form of the destruction of Jerusalem and the exile of large numbers of survivors to Babylon. This was understood by the prophets and many of the people as the judgment of God on the breaking of covenant moral mandates.

Although earlier prophets also addressed themes of hope and redemption beyond judgment the prophet we call Deutero-Isaiah (Isa 40–55) preached predominantly of hope and his message is less focused on renewed patterns of ethical conduct than the recovery of identity and character as God's people. By the time of the prophet's message the exiles from Jerusalem were in a second generation of exilic life in Babylon. Some had undoubtedly given up hope of a restored and renewed Israel as the people of God.[13]

Exile is less a forced change of geography than it is a crisis of identity and meaning. Psalm 137 despairs that "by the rivers of Babylon" they cannot "sing the LORD's song." The community of Lam 5:16–22 believed that because "we have sinned" God has "forgotten us completely." Into this community of resignation and hopelessness comes a prophetic voice of one who is indeed a singer of the LORD's song. This prophet proclaims a God who is not defined by judgment alone. Retributive justice is not the sole reality for the God this prophet preaches. There is hope and forgiveness and renewal as well. The prophet declares that exiles can reclaim their identity and relationship to God. They can be newly empowered to live out

---

13. For a fuller account of the exilic period, its social context, and theological witnesses, see Birch, *Let Justice Roll Down*, 280–320. See also Smith, *Religion of the Landless*; and Klein, *Israel in Exile*.

meaningful lives in the world as God's people. This in turn will allow them to become moral agents within the framework of Israel's historical tradition, to live once again as God's covenant people.

Almost immediately in the prophet's message he declares that the exiles are forgiven. "Comfort, O comfort my people, says your God; . . . she has served her term, her penalty is paid" (Isa 40:1–2). Even more directly and dramatically God says through the prophet "I, I am the One who blots out your transgressions for my own sake, and I will not remember your sins" (Isa 43:25). This is a crucial difference between exodus bondage and Babylonian captivity. Israel in Egypt is a story of victimization, but Israel in Babylon is a story of arrogance, greed, and idolatry. Both communities need God's deliverance but exiles need *God's forgiveness* as well. The good news announced by the prophet of the exile is that just as God took the initiative to bring Israel out of Egypt God has also taken the initiative to forgive and to no longer remember their sin. Not only that, but God claims to do this for God's own sake. When relationship is broken all need it restored and God announces the divine desire for restored relationship. There are no preconditions. Once again God models the moral response called for in the human community. Our tendency today is quite often to forgive with conditions. For instance, we will forgive, "If you won't do it again!" Or we want to make certain that those we forgive recognize their guilt. But the God who announces forgiveness in this prophet does not insist they look backward in guilt for sins committed in the past. Instead it is response to God's forgiveness that is called for and the response is repentance. The Hebrew word for repent is שוב which means to turn—to go another direction. Repentance is dynamic and forward-looking in new possibilities for restored relationship, to God and to others. The good news announced by the prophet's proclamation of God's forgiveness is that they are freed from guilt but called to repentance. What a freeing word to those who hope to rebuild community, in the prophet's time and our own.

Deutero-Isaiah also understood that exiles are often weighed down by the mere task of survival in the present. To rebuild community as moral agents requires reclaiming of a moral identity. So he called them to understand and reclaim the important dynamic *relationship between memory and vision*. They must reclaim a story with roots much older than the story of moral brokenness that led to exile. Their story is a story with a past and a future.

On the one hand, the prophet called them to remember who they are as the people of God with a long history of relationship to a God who has been with them through crises before. "Look to the rock from which you were hewn, and to the quarry from which you were dug. Look to Abraham your father and to Sarah who bore you . . ." (Isa 51:1b–2a). The prophet speaks in his proclamation of Noah (Isa 54:9) and David (Isa 55:3), and above all else, the exodus (Isa 43:15–17) and wilderness (Isa 40:3–5) traditions. If God brought them out before, God can do so again. Further, the God of exodus deliverance is also the God who created all things. Creation and exodus come together once again to make new life possible for God's people in Isa 51:9–10: "Awake, awake, put on strength, O arm of the LORD! Awake, as in days of old, the generations of long ago! Was it not you who cut Rahab in pieces, who pierced the dragon? Was it not you who dried up the sea, the waters of the great deep, who made the depths of the sea a way for the redeemed to cross over?"

But memory alone would not suffice. The prophet announces as God's word, "I am about to do a new thing, now it springs forth, do you not perceive it?" (Isa 43:19). To the non-singers by the rivers in Babylon the prophet declares, "Sing to the LORD a new song" (Isa 42:10). Memory of what God has done must be coupled with vision for what God yet can do. Neither alone will suffice. It is a foundation in memory on the one hand and confidence in the vision of God's future on the other hand that frees exiles from the tyranny of the present. This dynamic is as important to God's people now, in our own crises of exile, as it ever was before.

To claim this identity rooted in memory and vision is to become a different kind of moral community in the world. It is the foundation for trust that no barriers are too great and no grief is permanent for those who know the story of God's people and know that they are in relationship to that same God. "For your sake I will send to Babylon and break down all the bars, and the shouting of the Chaldeans will be turned to lamentations" (Isa 43:14).

In addition, the expansive portrait of God offered by the prophet to his exile generation means a serious call to identity as a people not fixed on its own parochial boundaries and conventions. If God is creator of all things and sovereign over all history then God may be found presenting new possibilities in surprising places. In Isa 44:28 and 45:1 the prophet announces to exiles that he sees God at work in Cyrus, the ruler of Persia, who will be the instrument to end their captivity. He even calls Cyrus "God's anointed." This may not have been a popular message (see Isa 45:9–13). But in 539 BCE it is Cyrus who marches into Babylon and allows the Jewish exiles to return to Jerusalem and rebuild the temple. The community that claims this prophetic tradition and passes it on as Scripture through generations down to our own is called to a moral identity as people convinced that God's power to make new, to make whole, to present new beginnings may manifest itself in unexpected and surprising ways that do not always carry the name of the religious community's endorsement.

There are, of course, many additional themes in the preaching of this exilic prophet, to say nothing of the whole of the prophetic tradition. It is significant for our self-understanding as moral communities that the prophets, whom we call speakers of God's word, are a part of our biblical inheritance. We are called both to listen for God's word and to proclaim it.

I propose that if we are concerned for a Christian ethics that is grounded in our biblical tradition we must claim the whole of that tradition. We must know and tell and live our story. We are shaped by our encounters with the whole of the Old Testament tradition. This story includes moments of failure to hear God's word and attempts to bend that word to suit human desires, which results in a broken covenant with God. But exactly these moments of failure are significant in our journey to be shaped as moral agents. I argue that through the life of faith that includes Bible reading, congregational preaching, devotional and critical study we must make the story of ancient Israel our own. We learn from Israel's faith and Israel's failures. We are inspired by leaders who embody God's will and speak God's word, and we are instructed by the many ways in which sin can create brokenness. Above all, we claim the Old Testament as a resource for Christian ethics because it is our only received channel of witness to the God who created us, called us, delivered us, covenanted with us, judged us, and redeemed us—in Israel's time and our own. Finally, we claim the mission of God's people to work for the restoration of a broken creation where human dignity is accorded to all as a foreshadowing of God's reign.

It is important to remember that this story contained in the Old Testament was the received biblical story of Jesus and all the New Testament writers who tell us his story. So they told us of the Messiah in the categories of the Hebrew biblical witness: Jesus Christ is a new creation, the example of the full humanity for which we were created. He is both a second Moses who proclaims God's word on the Mountain and is himself the Passover lamb through whom we are delivered from bondage to sin and death and summoned into a renewed covenant with God. And as exiles through our own sinfulness we are nevertheless offered forgiveness in God's own sacrifice. We are invited to reclaim a hopeful life as God's people called to be moral agents in a world where we remember that we all were given full human dignity in creation and we are now called as God's people and empowered to live toward the full and restored human dignity of all in a broken world moving toward the final consummation of God's mission to redeem the world.

BIBLIOGRAPHY

Barton, John. "Understanding Old Testament Ethics." *JSOT* 9 (1978) 44–64.

———. *Understanding Old Testament Ethics: Approaches and Explorations.* Louisville, KY: Westminster John Knox, 2003.

Birch, Bruce C. "Creation and the Moral Development of God in Genesis 1–11." In *And God Saw That It Was Good: Essays on Creation and God in Honor of Terence E. Fretheim*, edited by Frederick J. Gaiser and Mark A. Throntveit, 12–22. Word and World Supplement Series 5. St. Paul, MN: Word and World, Luther Seminary, 2006.

———. "Ethics in the OT." In *New Interpreter's Dictionary of the Bible*, Volume 2, edited by K. D. Sakenfeld, 338–48. Nashville, TN: Abingdon, 2007.

———. *Let Justice Roll Down: The Old Testament, Ethics, and Christian Life.* Louisville, KY: Westminster John Knox, 1991.

———. "Old Testament Narrative and Moral Address." In *Canon, Theology, and Old Testament Interpretation: Essays in Honor of Brevard S. Childs*, edited by Gene M. Tucker, David L. Petersen, and Robert R. Wilson, 75–91. Philadelphia: Fortress, 1988.

Birch, Bruce C., and Larry L. Rasmussen. *Bible and Ethics in the Christian Life.* Rev. ed. Minneapolis: Augsburg, 1989.

Birch, Bruce C., Walter Brueggemann, Terence E. Fretheim, and David L. Petersen. *A Theological Introduction to the Old Testament.* 2nd ed., 115–20. Nashville: Abingdon, 2005.

Fretheim, Terence E. *Exodus.* Interpretation Bible Commentaries. Louisville, KY: John Knox, 1991.

———. *The Suffering of God: An Old Testament Perspective.* Overtures to Biblical Theology. Philadelphia: Fortress, 1984.

Hanson, Paul D. *The People Called: The Growth of Community in the Bible.* San Francisco: Harper & Row, 1986.

Klein, Ralph W. *Israel in Exile: A Theological Interpretation.* Overtures to Biblical Theology. Philadelphia: Fortress, 1979.

Otto, Eckart. *Theologische Ethik des Alten Testaments.* Stuttgart: Kohlhammer, 1994.

Smith, Daniel L. *Religion of the Landless: The Social Context of the Babylonian Exile.* Bloomington, IN: Meyer-Stone, 1989.

Wenham, Gordon J. *Story as Torah: Reading Old Testament Ethically.* Edinburgh: T. & T. Clark, 2000.

PART 2

Violence

2

Violence, Mourning, Politics:
Rizpah's Lament in Conversation
with Judith Butler

L. Juliana Claassens,
Faculty of Theology, Stellenbosch University

INTRODUCTION

THE RATHER OBSCURE NARRATIVE told in 2 Samuel 21:1–14 of Rizpah, the widow of King Saul, lamenting the brutal death of her two sons as well as the sons of her stepdaughter Merab[1] divulges to us something we know all too well. Human beings are prone to injury, violence, and death—a reality clearly brought to our attention by the many instances of war and terror that in recent years have broken into our lives. The story of a mother losing

---

1. Cheryl Exum notes that the ancient witnesses are divided on whether Rizpah is lamenting in 2 Sam 21:8 for Merab or Michal's sons. Whereas the Masoretic text reads "Michal," other ancient texts have "Merab" which is the preferred reading since Merab was the wife of Adriel. Moreover, according to 2 Sam 6:23, Michal did not have any children, "Rizpah," 263.

her children as narrated in this biblical account is indeed reminiscent of the hundreds and thousands of mothers who on a daily basis are faced with the calamity of losing a child. As Judith Butler reminds us, "violence is surely a touch of the worst order, a way a primary human vulnerability to other humans is exposed in its most terrifying way, a way in which we are given over, without control, to the will of another, a way in which life itself can be expunged by the willful action of another."[2]

The story of Rizpah mourning over her sons moreover draws our attention to the link between violence and politics. The Gibeonites' demand to have seven of Saul's sons executed because Saul did not honor an old treaty that existed between Israel and the Gibeonites attests to how, in an endless cycle of violence, old feuds can return with a vengeance.[3]

However, what makes this narrative of Rizpah's lament unique, and in the past has captured the attention of interpreters who are sensitive to counter-voices in the text, is not first and foremost the narrative portrayal of violence and the petty politics that are responsible for this cycle of violence. What stands out in this narrative is the role of Rizpah, who is said to keep a six-month vigil "from the beginning of the harvest until the rains poured down on them from the heavens" (v. 10) for these victims of violence. She does not have much of a part in this narrative, at least not a speaking part, and her presence in the text constitutes little more than one sentence. Yet Rizpah emerges as one of the prime examples of female resistance in the face of violence in the biblical text. Her compelling narrative serves a powerful function of creating the space to consider timely topics that relate to how communities deal with trauma and particularly the link between "Violence, Mourning, and Politics" to reference the title of one of the chapters in Judith Butler's important work, *Precarious Life*. As part of a larger project on gender and human dignity, I will consider how the narrative of Rizpah lamenting not only for her own children, but also the children of others, may serve as a restorative reading in the context of the Old Testament, Ethics, and Human Dignity that forms the theme of this volume.

2. Butler, *Precarious Life*, 27–28.

3. This link between politics and violence is also evident in South Africa's painful history of apartheid. Gerald West writes in his article on Rizpah's lament how, when he read this narrative with students, some of his students were keen on identifying with the Gibeonites, arguing that the Gibeonites' demand for blood restitution evoked for them similar experiences of violence by the hand of the former apartheid regime. They could identify with the ensuing desire to see the perpetrators punished—in the South African context by reinstating the death penalty, "Reading on the Boundaries," 529.

FAILING TO MOURN

The narrative in 2 Sam 21:1–14 starts with the disturbing account of David trying to find a reason for the famine that for three years has ravaged the land.[4] Introducing God's voice in first person speech, the narrator divulges that the cause of the drought is divine displeasure regarding the blood-guilt resting on Saul's house because of his zealous attempts to wipe out the Gibeonites (vv. 1–2) despite the treaty that, according to Joshua 9, existed between the Gibeonites and Israel.[5] In order to restore the cosmic order so that it may rain again, David calls in the aggrieved Gibeonites who demand that the descendants of Saul be executed. Without as much as a hint of mental anguish, David complies with this request (v. 6), and Saul's two sons and five grandsons are brutally executed—the NRSV translates the Hebrew word וַיֹּקִיעֵם ("to tear apart") as "to be impaled" (v. 9). According to the LXX, an alternative translation would be "to scatter their bodies" which suggests dismemberment and that their bodies were left in the field in the wake of this violent massacre.[6]

The absence of a proper burial for Saul's sons points to the community's failure to duly mourn victims of violence. In her book, *Precarious Life*, Judith Butler contemplates this inability of a community to mourn loss with reference to the United States' response after 9/11 and the ensuing wars in Iraq and Afghanistan.[7] Butler argues that the community's failure to mourn is profoundly connected to a hierarchy of grief in that not all victims of violence are mourned equally. According to Butler, certain lives are

---

4. Marie-Theres Wacker notes that in the phrase, שָׁלֹשׁ שָׁנִים שָׁנָה אַחֲרֵי שָׁנָה (2 Sam 21:1), the repetition of "year" (שָׁנָה) points to the extent and the severity of a famine which continued year after year and which was responsible for the terrible suffering of many innocent people. With this introductory statement, the story is markedly placed in a context of suffering, "Rizpah," 551.

5. Wacker argues that according to the ancient Israelite worldview, the shedding of blood is intrinsically connected to famine. She refers to the Cain and Abel narrative in Gen 4:11–12 in which the ground is said to have opened its mouth to receive the blood of Abel with the result that, when Cain tills the ground, it will no longer yield to him its strength, "Rizpah," 551.

6. Gooder, "Remembering Rizpah," 26. In v. 14 it is said that the bodies of Saul's sons had to be gathered for burial, which perhaps supports the LXX translation.

7. Butler, *Precarious Life*, 28–29. Butler draws on Sigmund Freud's notion of "mourning and melancholia" according to which melancholia results from unresolved grief and an inability to mourn the loss of an object, person, or ideal. Cf. also Eng, "The Value of Silence," 87. I propose that the failure to bury the bones of Saul and his sons is symbolic of this inability to let go of the past.

not considered real so that "those who are unreal have, in a sense, already suffered the violence of derealization."[8] Referring to the United States' presence in Iraq and Afghanistan, Butler contemplates this act of derealization in terms of the thousands of nameless Iraqis and Afghanis who have died and who have gone unmourned:

> It is one thing to argue that first, on the level of discourse, certain lives are not considered lives at all, they cannot be humanized, that they fit no dominant frame for the human, and that their dehumanization occurs first, at this level, and that this level then gives rise to a physical violence that in some sense delivers the message of dehumanization that is already at work in the culture. If 200 000 Iraqi children were killed during the Gulf war, and its aftermath, do we have an image, a frame for any one of these lives, singly or collectively?[9]

The narrative in 2 Samuel 21 reflects something of this process of derealization when the sons of Saul for the most part go unnamed.[10] We know nothing of them, little more than that they were unfortunate enough to be the sons of Saul. Echoing Butler's probing questions with regard to the thousands of Iraqis and Afghanis who have died, one could well ask of Saul's sons: "Do they have names and faces, personal histories, family, favorite hobbies, slogans by which they live?"[11] One wonders whether this absence of a narrative frame that would humanize these individuals is not responsible for the fact that David so easily could give the sons of Saul over to be killed.[12] Their dehumanization furthermore is graphically realized by

---

8. Butler, *Precarious Life*, 33. Butler continues: "What, then, is the relation between violence and those lives considered as 'unreal'? Does violence effect that unreality? Does violence take place on the condition of that unreality?"

9. Butler, *Precarious Life*, 34.

10. Rizpah's two sons are named Armoni and Mephibosheth (v. 8), though not the five sons of Merab. The names of Rizpah's sons may be remembered due to Rizpah's selfless act of mourning, which as I will argue later in this essay, serves the function to memorialize them.

11. Butler, *Precarious Life*, 32.

12. David does spare the life of Mephibosheth, the son of Jonathan, because of an oath he made to Jonathan. It may be that the text contrasts in this instance David and Saul—David who does not break an oath he has made unlike Saul who in this text is said to have violated an oath with the Gibeonites, Wacker, "Rizpah," 552. On the other hand, it may be as Exum has argued that David spares Mephibosheth's life seeing that, due to his physical disability, he does not pose a threat to the throne, "Rizpah," 266. Cf. also Brenner, "I am the Glow," 127. I further would argue that in light of Judith Butler's point

their bodies violently being torn apart and then left in the field without being properly buried.

Judith Butler moreover is right that this failure to mourn, or even in certain situations, a prohibition to mourn can come back to haunt a community, leading to further violence.[13] Without a public act of grieving, there may be the temptation to engage in further violence to right past wrongs.[14] Butler contends that "when grieving is something to be feared, our fears can give rise to the impulse to resolve it quickly, to banish it in the name of an action invested with the power to restore the loss or return the world to a former order, or to reinvigorate a fantasy that the world formerly was orderly."[15]

In 2 Samuel 21, we see how this cycle of violence is associated with the famine-causing drought that in the narrator's mind serves as a symbol of the order in the world that had been upset by the injustice committed by Saul. Violence is thus committed in the name of restoring the disorder that has infected the land. It is moreover telling that if one goes back in narrative time, one finds that Saul himself and his son Jonathan also have not received a proper burial (1 Samuel 31).[16] It seems that this failure of the

---

of the importance of a narrative frame to foster a common connection, it may be that David's act of compassion is rooted in this personal connection to Mephibosheth's father Jonathan that serves to humanize him.

13. Judith Butler refers to Antigone's story in the context of the public mourning of violence: "There will be no public act of grieving (said Creon in Antigone). If there is a 'discourse,' it is a silent and melancholic one in which there have been no lives, and no losses; there has been no common bodily condition, no vulnerability that serves as the basis for an apprehension of our commonality; and there has been no sundering of that commonality," *Precarious Life*, 36.

14. Butler, *Precarious Life*, 33–34. Butler argues as follow: "If violence is done against those who are unreal, then, from the perspective of violence, it fails to injure or negate those lives since those lives are already negated. But they have a strange way of remaining animated and so must be negated again (and again). They cannot be mourned because they are always already lost or, rather, never 'were,' and they must be killed, since they seem to live on, stubbornly, in this state of deadness. Violence renews itself in the face of the apparent inexhaustibility of its object." Cf. also Eng who discusses this failure to mourn in terms of the United States' response after 9/11, "The Value of Silence," 88.

15. Butler, *Precarious Life*, 29–30.

16. According to 1 Sam 31:10, Saul and Jonathan's bodies were hanged upon the walls of the city of Bet Shean. After this, the local inhabitants of Jabesh Gilead buried their bodies in the area (vv. 11–13), Wacker, "Rizpah," 562. However, it is evident that this does not constitute a proper burial as Saul and Jonathan have not been gathered to their ancestors (Cf., e.g., Gen 25:8, 17; 49:29).

community to adequately mourn Saul and Jonathan indeed has come back to haunt the community in further expressions of violence.[17]

In addition, with the inhumane death of the sons of Saul there is the added danger that violence will renew itself in the face of the derealization of these victims in a war without end. It is furthermore significant, though, that the brutal deaths demanded by the Gibeonites as blood sacrifice does not have the desired effect of breaking the drought. It is at this point that Rizpah enters the story.

RESISTANCE AND LAMENT

The sum total of Rizpah's actions is to be found in 2 Sam 21:10. As the secondary wife or concubine (פִּלֶגֶשׁ in 2 Sam 21:11) of Saul, member of the disposed house of Saul, and now also childless widow, Rizpah has very little power.[18] She and the other women of her community could do nothing to stop the violent massacre. However, in v. 10 we read the following account of Rizpah's actions in resisting the violence that had befallen her people:

> Then Rizpah the daughter of Aiah took sackcloth, and spread it on a rock for herself, from the beginning of harvest until rain fell on them from the heavens; she did not allow the birds of the air to come on the bodies by day, or the wild animals by night.

In this singular verse, we see how Rizpah steps forward to mourn publicly the death of Saul's sons, protecting the bodies of her own sons as well as another mother's sons from predator birds for a period of six months. Rizpah employs the traditional mourning garb (הַשַּׂק) which she spreads out on the rock upon (or underneath) which she guards over the bodies of the deceased. For all the time that the parched earth is mourning due to the devastating drought, Rizpah mourns over her sons.[19]

17. Cheryl Exum writes that, although dead, Saul continues to dominate the story in 2 Samuel 21 when the violence Saul had committed against the Gibeonites returns with a vengeance in the brutal execution of his sons and grandsons, "Rizpah," 262. Even though David does call upon the mourning women to lament the deaths of Saul and Jonathan in addition to lamenting himself (2 Sam 1:11–27), the failure to bury these men is symbolic of the community's failure to adequately mourn their deaths.

18. Exum notes that the NRSV translation "concubine" for the Hebrew פִּלֶגֶשׁ is misleading as it suggests that Rizpah is not Saul's lawful wife. She proposes that a better translation would be "a legal wife of secondary rank." This designation, however, serves the purpose of indicating Rizpah's lowly status, "Rizpah," 261, 264.

19. Wacker, "Rizpah," 557–59. Wacker writes that the reference to the rains falling

There is a lot that the text does not say. For instance, Rizpah's voice is never heard—her actions mourning the death of these victims of violence are accompanied by silence.[20] It does not take much, though, to imagine this bereaved mother weeping silently as well as wailing at the top of her voice. So Rizpah's lament is to be understood in the context of women who through the ages have mourned the death of their loved ones. Luis Rivera-Pagán writes how, "in the wake of war," women's lament has served as a means of "resistance against the perennial proclivity to make force the arbiter of human conflicts."[21] Citing instances of professional wailing women in ancient Japan, Greece, and Mexico, as well as in modern-day India, Greece, and Iran, Kimberley Christine Patton, and John Stratton Hawley note the well-documented phenomenon in both ancient and contemporary societies of public and communal lamentation, especially weeping at funerals, being associated with women.[22] Also in the biblical traditions, we see a number of instances of female mourners, for instance, the daughters of Israel called to lament the deaths of Saul and Jonathan (2 Sam 1:24) as well as the wailing women in Jeremiah 9:17–20 whose tears and laments vocalize the pain and suffering the people experienced in the wake of the Babylonian invasion.[23]

An interesting example that helps one to visualize Rizpah mourning over her dead sons is found in Peter Paris' recollection of a funeral of a young man he once attended in Ghana. During this funeral, the casket was placed out in the open under the massive trees in the village. Paris describes how a grieving woman came forward and started to mourn the death of the young man:

from the heavens indicates an end to both the drought as well as Rizpah's mourning.

20. It is a question as to how to interpret Rizpah's silence. On the one hand, as Nancy Lee points out, "in regular Jewish mourning rituals, a period of silence is respected and observed," *Lyrics of Lament*, 12. On the other hand, her silence may be due to the failure of the biblical witness to recount Rizpah's action and speech. Cf. also Brenner who argues that Rizpah may be a silent witness, but hardly a passive one, "I am the Glow," 202.

21. Rivera-Pagán, "Woes of Captive Women," 130. Cf. also West who argues that Rizpah "was doing what women all over the world do, caring for the dead," "Reading on the Boundaries," 530. And Lee who notes that across cultures "the burden of this duty [is] on women," *Lyrics of Lament*, 152.

22. Patton and Hawley, "Introduction," 12.

23. For an exposition of the role of the wailing woman cf. Claassens, *Mourner, Mother, Midwife*, 18–30. Cf. also the central role of the daughter of Zion in voicing the people's suffering in the book of Lamentations in Lee, *Lyrics of Lament*, 31–32; Van Dijk-Hemmes, "Traces of Women's Texts," 83–86.

Her entire body seemed to be nearly broken by the weight of her sorrow. Throughout the service, she quietly and gracefully danced around the casket while reaching out her arms and hands in gentle gestures as she tried to embrace the casket. I have never before or since witnessed such mournful beauty. The entire liturgy and all of the participants seemed to be drawn into the aura of that grieving woman's physical movements as her faith confronted the cold presence of death with sadness and love.[24]

Also the content of Rizpah's lament is hidden from us. In her book, *Lyrics of Lament*, Nancy Lee has collected laments from all over the world, both ancient as well as modern, which helps us to contemplate the sorrow this mother may have been voicing while guarding the bodies of her sons. For instance, in the book of Lamentations one reads of the Daughter of Zion voicing the suffering of the people in the wake of the terrible violence they have experienced at the hand of the Babylonian Empire:

> O LORD, look at my affliction, for the enemy has triumphed! . . .
> Look, O LORD, and see how worthless I have become.
> Is it nothing to you, all you who pass by? Look and see if there is
> any sorrow like my sorrow (Lam 1:9c, 11c–12).

And in an early Islamic lament, Rahab mourns the death of her husband Husayn:

> He who was light, shining, is murdered;
> Murdered in Karbala, and unburied.
> Descendant of the Prophet, may God reward you well
> May you be spared judgment on the day when deeds are weighed:
> For you were to me as a mountain, solid in which I could take refuge;
> And you treated us always with kindness, and according to religion.
> O who shall speak now for the orphans, for the petitioners;
> By whom shall all these wretched be protected, in whom shall they take refuge?[25]

---

24. Paris, "When Feeling Like a Motherless Child," 119. Cf. also Athalya Brenner who imagines vividly how Rizpah, who is called the daughter of Ayah, meaning "falcon," could speak to the birds during her lonely quest in protecting her sons bodies from further desecration, "I am the Glow," 122, 131.

25. Cited in Lee, *Lyrics of Lament*, 38.

In these laments, we see some common features found in lament songs across cultures that offers an interpretative framework for Rizpah's lament. For instance, Lee describes shared motifs such as a complaint about the tragic death of a loved one, reference to the death and how the person died, especially if it was due to violence, expressions of sorrow and weeping. In the second example cited above, one also sees the direct address to the dead, which includes praise for the deceased as well as a plea to the deity.[26]

Rizpah's lament in the wake of the terrible violence that has destroyed the lives of her sons and the sons of Merab may on all accounts seem futile. Her lament most certainly cannot bring her sons back to life. And yet as Judith Butler points out, "[t]o grieve, and to make grief itself into a resource for politics, is not to be resigned to inaction, but it may be understood as the slow process by which [an individual] develop[s] a point of identification with suffering itself."[27] Rizpah's lament thus offers us some important perspectives regarding the nature of resistance in the face of violence. First, by lamenting, Rizpah transcends the dignity-destroying effects of violence, so attesting to the universal truth that to be human means to resist those forces that seek to assault, violate or obscure one's human dignity.[28] The very act of resisting as exemplified in Rizphah's lament, even though it may not change the victim's situation in any decisive way, is hence a sign that this person is maintaining some basic sense of what it means to be human. As Nancy Lee writes: "Lament in essence, provides a cathartic vehicle for human beings to express all aspects of suffering and to help maintain the value and dignity of one's humanity under hardship if possible."[29] In very difficult circumstances as suggested by Rizpah's wake in the wilderness, Rizpah shows tremendous courage in the face of violence.

Second, Rizpah's lament serves as an act of silent public protest regarding the injustice committed; as a testimony to the futility of violence

---

26. Ibid., 52. Lee moreover shows how some laments may also include "a call for justice, revenge or a curse."

27. Butler, *Precarious Life*, 30.

28. In her book, *Plantations and Death Camps: Religion, Ideology, and Human Dignity*, Beverly Eileen Mitchell argues that in the worst hovels of human existence, such as the extreme degradation of human beings experienced by the Jews in the extermination camps during the Holocaust and by the African-American slaves on the plantations in the South, to be human means to express indignation at having one's humanity denied or one's dignity assaulted, 4.

29. Lee, *Lyrics of Lament*, 27.

that affects the community as a whole.[30] Gerald West, reading Rizpah's lament in terms of James Scott's[31] work on passive resistance, furthermore argues that Rizpah's lament constitutes a hidden transcript over against the dominant ideologies and theologies of those in power.[32] According to West, Rizpah's lament constitutes a prime example of female resistance in that she was "caring for the dead while and because men in power did not care for the living."[33] Moreover, Marie-Theres Wacker notes that Rizpah engages in an act of resistance, not only against the wild animals and birds but also against David.[34]

Rizpah's act of resistance, though, is not without risk. As Judith Butler writes regarding the classic story of Antigone, which is also cited by Cheryl Exum[35] in connection with Rizpah's lament: "Antigone, risking death herself by burying her brother against the edict of Creon, exemplified the political risks in defying the ban against public grief during times of increased sovereign power and hegemonic national unity."[36] Those in power know all too well that lament is dangerous indeed. These "weapons of the weak," to quote Scott's well-known description of hidden transcripts such as women's lament, may unleash a tidal wave of voices demanding change and an end to the abuse of power.[37] We thus see how Rizpah continues day after day in her self-imposed duty of mourning the violent death of her sons, so becom-

30. Lee argues as follow: "Lament is . . . a call to bring attention to injustice an anguished plea for respite and consolation, an appeal for intervention not only to one's deity, but to one's community and to the world community," *Lyrics of Lament*, 27.

31. Scott, *Weapons of the Weak*; Scott, *Domination and the Arts of Resistance*.

32. West, "Reading on the Boundaries," 530. Passive resistance can be defined as acts of defiance by the oppressed which, in contrast to aggressive or violent resistance, are rooted in everyday actions that at first glance may seem to be trivial and insignificant, but that are actually quite creative and potentially liberating. Cf. Claassens, "Resistance, Passive."

33. West, "Reading on the Boundaries," 530. Cf. also Brenner who views Rizpah's lament in terms of a long tradition of nonverbal protest, "I am the Glow," 126–27.

34. Wacker, "Rizpah," 557–58.

35. Cf. Cheryl Exum who has read the story of Rizpah in terms of the story of Antigone mourning the death of her brothers, "Rizpah," 261.

36. Butler, *Precarious Life*, 46. Cf. Bonnie Honig's critique of Butler's application of Antigone's narrative as a basis for a new (mortalist) humanism, "Antigone's Two Laws," 8–10. She argues: "Against those who seek in lamentation a universal humanism of sound and cry, I have argued that Antigone's dirge is a partisan political intervention," 18. She furthermore points out that "Antigone is not a mother: she refuses to be one and laments the fact that she will never be one," 5.

37. Lee, *Lyrics of Lament*, 24.

ing an enduring example of embodied lament that moves the community to face the tragic death of the sons of Saul and to adequately mourn their deaths.

Third, Rizpah's lament constitutes a powerful means of resisting the derealization experienced by Saul's sons. Her lament serves as a type of obituary for these victims of violence—her six-month vigil preventing her sons as well as the sons of Merab to be completely erased.[38] Judith Butler writes as follow about the nature of an obituary:

> "[Obituary] is a means by which life becomes, or fails to become, a publically grievable life, an icon for national self-recognition, the means by which a life becomes noteworthy. . . . The matter is not a simple one, for, if a life is not grievable, it is not quite a life and is not worth a note. It is already the unburied, if not the unburiable."[39]

By means of Rizpah's public grief over these seven victims of violence, the lives of her sons and her stepsons are recognized and prevented from falling into oblivion. As in the lament of Rahab mourning the death of her husband cited above, one could well imagine Rizpah supplying details in her lament regarding the lives these young men have lived, serving the function of reclaiming their humanity once more. The following contemporary lament by an anonymous Chinese mother after her son was shot at Tiananmen Square makes this point well. In the final stanza of "Crying over Child: To the Child Killed by Nine Gun Shots," one of the laments collected by Lee, the bereaved mother voices her shock and anguish at seeing her son shot:

> They say you were a rioter,
> They said
> You'd sabotage the 20-million lives-
> built great palace.
> Nevertheless
> Mum knows
> You were just a naïve child
> Pulling Mum's hand yesterday
> Urged Mum to take you to the park.[40]

38. Brenner, "I am the Glow," 127. In first person speech, Brenner supplies Rizpah's voice: "I couldn't save the boys from their fate but I could save their memory, especially the memory of my own sons. Why even their names are recorded, unlike the names of Merab's sons."

39. Butler, *Precarious Life*, 34.

40. "Crying over Child: To the Child Killed by Nine Gun Shots," cited in Lee, *Lyrics*

Imagining Rizpah's lament in terms of mothers like this Chinese mother remembering her dead son as a little boy serves as an alternative narrative frame through which the humanity of these victims of violence are reclaimed. Moreover, as we will see in the following section, this act of resisting dehumanization has an important transformative effect that is responsible for this narrative to serve as a restorative reading.

MOURNING AND TRANSFORMATION

Rizpah's lament is significant beyond the singular verse narrative space afforded to her actions.[41] We see how her six-month vigil lamenting the brutal death of her children has a transformative effect on all who witnessed her resolve to effectively mourn the violence that had destroyed the lives of Saul's sons and grandsons. As Judith Butler describes this link between mourning and transformation: "In the asking, in the petition, we have already become something new, since we are constituted by virtue of the address, a need and desire for the Other that takes place in language in the broadest sense, one without which we could not be. . . . It is to solicit a becoming, to instigate a transformation, to petition the future always in relation to the Other."[42]

So we see how God hears her cries and sees her lament when it finally starts to rain.[43] As we have noted before, the rain is not connected with the blood sacrifice demanded by the Gibeonites, but closely linked with Rizpah's lament. According to v. 10, Rizpah conducted her solitary vigil until it started to rain again. The divine response of giving rain again as symbol of the order that has been restored is thus associated with the community's satisfactory mourning of the victims of violence—a process initiated by Rizpah's lament.[44]

---

of Lament, 36.

41. Exum notes that Rizpah's action is "absolutely pivotal, for it changes the entire course of events," "Rizpah," 261. She argues: "The causal nexus between divine displeasure, atonement, and divine appeasement set up by the story is abruptly broken by Rizpah's awesome display of the proper reverence due the dead," 267.

42. Butler, *Precarious Life*, 44.

43. West argues that "the silent cries of Rizpah and the dead were heard by God," 530. So we see how "God responds first, and the rain falls on Rizpah and the dead (v. 10a). David then also responds, recognizing, we hope, another more accountable, responsible, and compassionate theology," "Reading on the Boundaries," 531.

44. Exum, "Rizpah," 267. God's act of giving rain again, may also be a sign of

Moreover, Rizpah's lament also has a profoundly transformative effect on King David.[45] It is significant that in response to Rizpah's vigil for her sons as well as the sons of Merab, King David finally is obliged to respect the dignity of the dead by giving these victims of violence a decent burial. With this act, something of the humanity of Saul's sons is recovered. It is moreover significant that David also, after all this time, decides to bury the bones of King Saul and his son Jonathan when he heard what Rizpah had done (vv. 11–12). Rizpah's display of her grief is thus helping David to also deal with the community's failure to adequately mourn the tragedies of the past.

Judith Butler writes that at the heart of mourning's ability to effect transformation on an individual as well as on a political level is the recognition of a common human vulnerability. It is, on the one hand, the realization that as humans we are all profoundly vulnerable to violence that may eradicate our being; however, on the other hand, as vulnerable human beings, we are also dependent on the other for the physical support of our lives.[46]

Read in terms of Judith's Butler's thoughts on mourning and transformation, one could argue that this ability to forge a common vulnerability is already modelled by Rizpah. So it is significant that Rizpah's lament extends beyond her own sons also to another woman's sons. By weeping also for Merab's children, Rizpah embodies an important principle voiced by Judith Butler, i.e., being able to recognize the suffering of another.[47]

Moreover, Gerald West also imagines that Rizpah "could not have survived day and night, month after month, without the support of her sisters from other sectors of the society." He ventures to say that perhaps even Merab (Michal) (the mother of the other sons mourned by Rizpah) was

---

transformation in God who up till this point has been consistently involved in punishing Saul—all of Saul's male relations met untimely deaths and Michal suffered the terrible fate of dying childless, Exum, "Rizpah," 266.

45. Athalya Brenner describes Rizpah as a tool for educating David, "Rizpah [Re]Membered," 207–8. Cf. also Gooder, "Remembering Rizpah," 28.

46. Butler, *Precarious Life*, 31. Cf. Lord Eames, the co-chair of the Consultative Group on Irish Reconciliation's powerful statement that expresses this humanistic promise that is rooted in the universal expression of the fact of mortality and the cry of pain: "There is no difference in a mother's tears." Cited in Honig, "Antigone's Two Laws," 5.

47. Butler writes: "If vulnerability is one precondition for humanization, and humanization takes place differently through variable norms of recognition, then it follows that vulnerability is fundamentally dependent on existing norms of recognition if it is to be attributed to any human subject," *Precarious Life*, 43.

among those who acted in solidarity with Rizpah, sustaining her through her six-month vigil.[48]

This ability to recognize a common vulnerability is vital in a conversation on recovering human dignity in the face of violence. According to Butler, the recognition of this common vulnerability is a precondition for humanization that is greatly important in a conversation on ethics within the international political arena. As Butler argues:

> From the subsequent experience of loss and fragility, however, the possibility of making different kinds of ties emerges. Such mourning might (or could) effect a transformation in our sense of international ties that would crucially rearticulate the possibility of democratic political culture here and elsewhere.[49]

Finally, Rizpah's lament is significant in that it offers an important way out of violence. Her lament over the tragedy that had befallen her people breaks the cycle of violence that for a very long time existed between the Israelites and the Gibeonites.[50] In the biblical traditions there are many laments that call for revenge and further violence to settle past scores. For instance, in Ps 137:8–9, we read the brutal wish that the heads of the babies of the Babylonians be dashed against the rocks.[51] Even though we do not know the content of Rizpah's lament during her six-month vigil, the act of burying the sons of Saul's bodies together with their father and brother Jonathan does signal an end to violence and serves as a powerful symbol of the community dealing with its grief.[52] In this regard, Judith Butler argues

48. West continues: "But maybe not. Merab, like the leaders of the Gibeonites, may have actively embraced the dominant theology of retribution and death," "Reading on the Boundaries," 531.

49. Butler, *Precarious Life,* 40. Butler continues: "We make the claim, however, precisely because it is not taken for granted, precisely because it is not, in every instance, honored. Vulnerability takes on another meaning at the moment it is recognized, and recognition wields the power to reconstitute vulnerability," 43.

50. Cf. also Emanuel Levinas who ends his reading of 2 Samuel 21 not with the Gibeonites' cruel demand for justice, but with Rizpah's sacrifice, Mole, "Cruel Justice," 266.

51. With regard to what she calls the "poetry of revenge" in Jeremiah, Kathleen O'Connor writes that these literary expressions for revenge in the face of trauma constitutes a healthy part of the recovery process as it creates space for healing to take place, *Jeremiah,* 119. Cf. also Nancy Lee's warning that such texts could be dangerous if they are used to sanction socio-political violence, *Lyrics of Lament,* 184.

52. Cf. also Wacker who argues that this burial of Saul and Jonathan's bones suggests a reunification of the house of the first king of Israel, Saul, [in German "eine postmortale

that what is at stake in reframing past events in order to change the world in the direction of non-violence is the recognition of a common human vulnerability.[53] Butler writes:

> But perhaps there is some other way to live such that one becomes neither affectively dead nor mimetically violent, a way out of the circle of violence altogether. This possibility has to do with demanding a world in which bodily vulnerability is protected without therefore being eradicated and with insisting on the line that must be walked between the two.[54]

It is thus by reading one's own suffering through the lens of someone else that we may derive a principle by which we vow to protect others from the kinds of violence we have suffered by, as Butler suggests, challenging the notion that "certain human lives are more vulnerable than others, and thus certain human lives are more grievable than others."[55]

CONCLUSION

The narrative of Rizpah's lament may serve as a restorative reading in that it encourages the reader to contemplate the pain felt by people around the world who have lost their sons and daughters to the infinite cycle of violence. This narrative as told in 2 Samuel 21 opens up space for the reader to make sense of other traumatic experiences—the dialogical exchange with other situations of trauma making it possible to recognize connections between other individuals and groups suffering violence.[56] In this regard, it is interesting to take note of the reception history of Rizpah's lament. For instance, Athalya Brenner cites a poem by an Australian poet, Henry Kendall,

---

Vereinigung des Hauses Sauls, des ersten Königs Israels]", "Rizpah," 563. Only with this act of restoration can there once again be peace in the land. Cf. also the last verse of this pericope in which it is said that "After that, God heeded supplications for the land" (2 Sam 21:14).

53. Butler, *Precarious Life*, 17.

54. Ibid., 42.

55. Ibid., 30. Cf. also the application of Butler's thought by Saal, "Regarding the Pain of Self and Other," 451–76.

56. Cf. Saal's interesting example of Jonathan Safran Foer's novel *Extremely Loud and Incredibly Close* that in an act of trauma, transfer seeks to read the trauma of 9/11 in terms of the bombing of Dresden during the Second World War. Engaging Judith Butler's work on "Violence, Mourning, and Politics," Saal contemplates how successful this narrative transfer is in Foer's novel, "Regarding the Pain of Self and Other," 464–65.

who in the nineteenth century spoke about the Rizpahs of these modern days "who've lost their households through no sins of theirs, on bloody fields and in the pits of war." Making a connection with the Civil War that "shook America for five long years," Kendall cites Rizpah who like Rachel in Rama wept for her children and refused to be comforted.[57] And Nancy Lee cites a number of modern-day protest movements, for instance, the Women in Black movement that started in 1988 in Jerusalem with a group of Jewish and Palestinian women who, clothed in black, silently stood together in public, protesting war, death, and violence.[58]

Rizpah's courageous act of resistance thus serves as a model of resisting violence that continues to violate the dignity of men, women, and children in contested spaces all across the world.[59] As Archbishop Desmond Tutu's lament voices this yearning for dignity in a situation of dehumanization as we have seen in apartheid South Africa. In a sermon on the Daughter of Zion's lament cited earlier, he exclaims:

> Your dignity is not just rubbed in the dust. It is trodden underfoot and spat on. Our people are being killed as if they were but flies. Is that nothing to you who pass by? What must we say that we have not said? God give us eloquence such that the world will hear that all we want is to be recognized for what we are—human beings created in your image."[60]

---

57. Cited in Brenner, "Rizpah [Re]Membered," 223. Saal raises an interesting point regarding questions of agency in terms of situations of trauma. She says that "while a wound is wound regardless of nationality, religion or ideological conviction. . . . It does matter who inflicts it and for what reasons," "Regarding the Pain of Self and Other," 469.

58. Lee describes silent laments of the Tiananmen Mother's Campaign which are a prime example of embodied lament, *Lyrics of Lament*, 34–35. Cf. also the Black Sash movement's silent protest against the apartheid regime in South Africa, as described by Denise Ackermann in her essay, "On Hearing and Lamenting," 47–56.

59. Saal warns though of a too facile appropriation of other's suffering, as the particularities of a situation of suffering may be lost, "Regarding the Pain of Self and Other," 456. In this regard, Bonnie Honig critiques of attempts that make a connection between contemporary mourning mothers and classic figures such as Antigone (I would also add Rizpah). Honig argues that such an identification creates a new universalism which shows little regard for the particularities of both literature and politics, "Antigone's Two Laws," 2. Nonetheless, Honig does admit that even though "Antigone's words are political, that may leave intact the mortalist-humanist claim that lamentation accesses or stages a commonality that eludes politics and on which a new (post)politics or ethics should be built," 18.

60. Cited in Lee, *Lyrics of Lament*, 167.

With these words in mind, Rizpah's silent lament so long ago over the bodies of her dead sons is echoed in every new plea for resisting violence and recovering the human dignity of those victims whose dignity has been "rubbed in the dust," trodden underfoot," and "spat [up]on." Ultimately the restorative potential of Rizpah's lament is situated in its ability to inspire readers centuries later to continue working for a less violent and more humane world.[61]

BIBLIOGRAPHY

Ackermann, Denise M. "On Hearing and Lamenting: Faith and Truth Telling." In *To Remember and to Heal: Theological and Psychological Reflections on Truth and Reconciliation*, edited by H. Russel Botman and Robin M. Petersen, 47–56. Cape Town: Human & Rousseau, 1996.

Brenner, Athalya. "I am the Glow: Rizpah Daughter of Ayah." In *I Am: Biblical Women Tell Their Own Stories*, edited by Athalya Brenner, 120–32. Minneapolis: Fortress, 2004.

———. "Rizpah [Re]Membered: 2 Samuel 1–14 and Beyond." In *Performing Memory in Biblical Narrative and Beyond*, edited by Athalya Brenner and Frank H. Polak, 207–27. Sheffield, UK: Sheffield Phoenix, 2009.

Butler, Judith. *Precarious Life: The Powers of Mourning and Violence*. London: Verso, 2004.

Claassens, L. Juliana. *Mourner, Mother, Midwife: Reimagining God's Liberating Presence*. Louisville, KY: Westminster John Knox, 2012.

———. "Resistance, Passive." In *Oxford Encyclopaedia of the Bible and Ethics*. ed. Robert L. Brawley; Oxford: Oxford University Press, 2015.

Eng, David L. "The Value of Silence." *Theatre Journal* 54/1 (2002) 85–94.

Exum, Cheryl. "Rizpah." *Word & World* 17/3 (1997) 260–68.

Gooder, Paula. "Remembering Rizpah." *Sojourners Magazine* 33/1 (2004) 24–28.

Honig, Bonnie. "Antigone's Two Laws: Greek Tragedy and the Politics of Humanism." *New Literary History* 41/1 (2010) 1–33.

Lee, Nancy. *Lyrics of Lament: From Tragedy to Transformation*. Minneapolis, MN: Fortress, 2010.

Mitchell, Beverly Eileen. *Plantations and Death Camps: Religion, Ideology, and Human Dignity*. Minneapolis, MN: Fortress, 2009.

Mole, Gary. "Cruel Justice, Responsibility, and Forgiveness: On Levinas's Reading of the Gibeonites." *Modern Judaism* 31/3 (2011) 253–71.

O'Connor, Kathleen M. *Jeremiah: Pain and Promise*. Minneapolis, MN: Fortress, 2011.

Paris, Peter J. "When Feeling Like a Motherless Child." In *Lament: Reclaiming Practices in Pulpit, Pew, and Public Square*, edited by Sally A. Brown and Patrick D. Miller, 111–20. Louisville, KY: Westminster John Knox, 2001.

61. Rivera-Pagán, "Woes of Captive Women," 130. Lee argues as follows: "Voicing loss and sorrow also may help to curtail future violence, injustice, and human and social disintegration. Singing our sorrow and lament is necessary for our own faith and our diverse faiths, and ironically, for all of our efforts at serving and healing the world," *Lyrics of Lament*, 16.

Patton, Kimberley C., and John S. Hawley. *Holy Tears: Weeping in the Religious Imagination.* Princeton, NJ: Princeton University Press, 2005.

Rivera-Pagán, Luis N. "Woes of Captive Women: From Lament to Defiance in Times of War." In *Lament: Reclaiming Practices in Pulpit, Pew, and Public Square,* edited by Sally A. Brown and Patrick D. Miller, 121–34. Louisville, KY: Westminster John Knox, 2005.

Saal, Ilka. "Regarding the Pain of Self and Other: Trauma Transfer and Narrative Framing in Jonathan Safran Foer's *Extremely Loud and Incredibly Close." Modern Fiction Studies* 57/3 (2011) 451–76.

Scott, James C. *Domination and the Arts of Resistance: Hidden Transcripts.* New Haven, CT: Yale University Press, 1990.

———. *Weapons of the Weak: Everyday Forms of Peasant Resistance.* New Haven, CT: Yale University Press, 1985.

Van Dijk-Hemmes, Fokkelien. "Traces of Women's Texts in the Hebrew Bible." In *On Gendering Texts: Female and Male Voices in the Hebrew Bible,* edited by Athalya Brenner and Fokkelien Van Dijk-Hemmes, 17–109. Biblical Interpretation Series 1. Leiden: Brill, 1993.

Wacker, Marie-Theres. "Rizpah oder: Durch Trauer-Arbeit zur Versöhnung: Anmerkungen zu 2 Sam 21, 1–14." In *Textarbeit: Studien zu Texten und ihrer Rezeption aus dem Alten Testament und der Umwelt Israels. Festschrift für Peter Weimar zur Vollendung seines 60. Lebensjahres mit Beiträgen von Freunden , Schülern und Kollegen,* edited by Klaus Kiesow and Thomas Meurer, 545–67. Münster: Ugarit-Verlag, 2003.

West, Gerald. "Reading on the Boundaries: Reading 2 Samuel 21:1–14 with Rizpah." *Scriptura* 63 (1997) 527–37.

3

Outrageous Terror and Trying Texts:
Restoring Human Dignity in Judges 19–21

Douglas Lawrie,
Department of Religion and Theology,
University of Western Cape

BETWEEN IDEOLOGY AND INDETERMINACY

I DOUBT WHETHER ANY woman can read Judges 19–21 without outrage; if some men can, I shudder. Mieke Bal calls the rape of the concubine in Judges 19 "the most horrible scene in the entire Bible."[1] It is so horrible—and the horror is so well portrayed—that one may overlook that the chapters that follow are hardly better. In chapter 20, what could have been an exercise in justice becomes an indiscriminate slaughter. According to Judg 20:48, the avenging mob killed everything they encountered in Gibeah—from men to animals.[2] The next chapter confirms that this included all the women. By

---

1. Bal, "Between Altar and Wandering Rock," 230.

2. The verse is difficult and MT may be corrupt (see BHS), but the meaning is not unclear.

a grim irony some of the conceivably guilty Benjaminite men escaped but none of the obviously innocent women. This orgy of killing is supposedly an act of piety undergirded by a grotesque parody of religious observance.[3]

In chapter 21 the blood-gorged Israelites apparently come to their senses. They are shocked to find that they have all but exterminated their Benjaminite brothers. That they have dealt more thoroughly with their Benjaminite sisters seems to them to be merely a technical problem awaiting "imaginative" solutions—that involve further killings of men and rapes of women. If this is the naked face of patriarchy, the case is closed: "against it by lot!"[4] (Judg 20:9b, MT).

When employing ideological criticism to interpret this outrageous text, the ideological critic first has to consult the textual oracle. Judges 19–21 is probably not a unitary text, and there is no clear consensus about its literary history.[5] Having met ideology in the shape of patriarchy, the ideological critic is thus confronted by indeterminacy: a text that is not self-explanatory and may not be one text but several.[6] Decisions about the unity and literary history of the text sometimes—not invariably—influence one's understanding of the author's ideology; similarly, a particular view of the author's ideology sometimes influences one's decisions about what is and is not secondary.

The easy way to wed ideological criticism and theories of indeterminacy is to say that texts, underdetermined in themselves, must yield to the intentions of readers. If, as a feminist, I wish to unmask the ideology of the text, the text cannot resist my resisting reading.[7] The trouble is that

---

3. This is noted by most scholars. See, for instance, Boling, *Judges*, 277, 286; Crüsemann, *Widerstand*, 164–65; Eynikel, *Judges 19–21*, 113–14.

4. As indicated by a more or less literal translation of Judg 20:9b (MT), with the sole change being that the Hebrew uses the feminine (for the city). Most translators follow the LXX which adds a verb, but the MT has the *lectio difficilior* which is followed by the other translations and offers a more compelling reading. The Greek seems to be a translation *ad sensum*.

5. It is usually accepted that chapter 19 is a unitary narrative with only minor additions; however, some scholars regard chapters 20–21 as secondary, and others only chapter 21. Cf. Jüngling, *Richter 19*, 245–80; Becker, *Richterzeit*, 266–96.

6. Eryl Davies traces the parentage of feminist hermeneutics to reader-response criticism and ideological criticism, *The Dissenting Reader*, 32–81. The same bloodline runs through much of contemporary hermeneutics.

7. Roland Barthes, "Death of the Authors," cedes all authority over the text to the readers, but, as Butler, "Future of Reading," 247, points out, he elides ideology. Stanley Fish, who joins the two strands in another way, is accused by Eagleton, *Ideology*, 169, of

"unmasking," since it belongs to a different discursive formation, becomes indeterminate in this context.[8] Am I unmasking the text to show its hidden face or am I masking it in order to show my suitably beautified face? How can I subvert if I cannot tell the bottom from the top or read against the grain unless I know how the grain runs?[9]

Loosely used, terms like "dissenting reader" and "resisting reader" confound the differing roles of the reader and the critic. If I dissent or resist as reader, I cannot read: I dissent from the reading process and resist reading. Having read, I can, as critic, dissent from what I have read and resist the implications of my reading. As a critic, that is, as a judge. For when it comes to ideology and ethics, the excuse that criticism amounts to analysis, a technical operation performed on a lifeless object, will not do. To condemn an impersonal ideology because it causes harm is like condemning a flood because it does the same. If ideology infects us in ways beyond our control, condemning ideologues is like condemning lepers.

That I am biased in many ways, some of them unknown to me, I do not deny. If, however, I am to act as judge in matters involving my biases, I may wish to resist my biases and, for a moment, dissent from myself. Being human, I may not be very successful; being human, I can give it a try. Only when my suspicions about myself fail me can I begin to speak of my ethics—and then without the assurance that my ethics is superior to that of another. In both cases some arguments will play a role, but when it comes to ethically irreconcilable positions, arguments too fail. I have to appeal—and be open to appeals—to honor and shame. And it is decidedly a matter of honor to award my interlocutor a voice.

BRINGING THE AUTHOR TO LIFE

Though not as fiendishly difficult as Judges 20, Judges 21 presents problems that cannot be solved without some speculation. No solution is entirely satisfactory. Is the entire chapter secondary? Have two different accounts

---

making the self "the helplessly determined product of history, a mere puppet of its social interests."

8. On this inconsistency in Fish particularly, see Tompkins, "Introduction," xxiii, and, more generally, Appiah, *Tolerable Falsehoods*, 66–72.

9. Unless we say, as David Hume did in a similar context, "Carelessness and inattention alone can afford us any remedy. For this reason I rely entirely on them," *Treatise of Human Nature*, 268.

been conflated and, if so, do they come from different times and carry different intentions? Opinions differ. In addition, many scholars reckon with the presence of additions, though they differ regarding the extent and location of these. I am inclined to think that chapter 21 belongs with the rest of the narrative and that two accounts have been editorially combined (with minor changes to v. 14 and v. 22), but that essentially the same voice intention animates both.[10] The additions I ascribe to the priestly glossator who battled to make sense of the basic text. For instance, the second oath (v. 5) seems to be an addition to justify the cynical decision in v. 8. Note the awkward break caused by the placing of v. 5. The reference to Bethel is probably also secondary. Though I can muster arguments for my views, the evidence is hardly conclusive.[11]

Therefore I start with what cannot be excised from the narrative without changing it completely. Having practically eradicated the Benjaminites, the Israelites have second thoughts. In a fit of supposed compassion (vv. 6, 15), they try to ensure the survival of their "brothers" by providing them with wives. Though they had heedlessly massacred innocent Benjaminite women, they have qualms about breaking a rash oath. Thus a fresh batch of victims has to be found. What distinguishes the second genocide—"exterminate them!"—from the first is that the survivors will not be those who escape but those selected for rape. All other women, it is said explicitly, are to be killed. The second plan, which involves no killing, also treats women as mere objects. In verse 22 the hypocrisy of the elders is patent. They evade a legitimate complaint from the protectors of the maidens, invoke compassion for the Benjaminites but not for the women, and give the assurance that the oath has not formally been breached. Perhaps the right hand will not find out what the left hand is doing. Then both Benjaminites and Israelites return in peace to their inheritance—mission accomplished.

What human person can write like this? The assumption that the author is morally blind does not help: even a depraved but minimally

10. A similar view is held by Guillaume, *Waiting for Josiah*, 224, who notes that both endings are anti-Benjaminite. In other respects his reading does insufficient justice to the irony of the composition.

11. The most compelling evidence is negative. Perhaps different old traditions were combined (particularly in Judges 21) and probably the combined text received fairly extensive additions (particularly in Judges 20). But how could a fairly random process of editing have resulted in a narrative that not only appears coherent in plot, but contains an intricate network of ironies and links *across the chapters*? Kamuf's summary of the narrative, "Author of a Crime," 192–94, shows that this is apparent to a literary reader who is not a specialist in this field.

intelligent person would see that rape and murder cannot be corrected by multiplying rapes and murders, and that disproportionate revenge has no religious sanction. The postulate of an author so steeped in patriarchy as to disregard completely the lot of women fares no better. It is hard to see the author of these chapters as a naïve dupe, for the writing suggests careful rhetorical planning. Every horror is calculated to count against Saul,[12] against the northern tribes generally, *and* against those who rejected the Davidic monarchy in favor of a stateless society.[13] The rape of the nameless, voiceless concubine works rhetorically for the author *because it is abominable.* On the assumption that "concubines, being less than human, are fair game,"[14] the mud slung at Saul's city would not have stuck. Similarly, when the Levite lies about the events before the assembly (Judg 20:4–7), readers know that he is lying, but are not surprised. He had revealed his character before.

We have every reason to look for a subtle author in these chapters, regardless of whether, in our view, the subtlety is employed to good or bad ends. If the voice behind chapter 19 is still speaking in chapter 21, we may detect moral defects, but should postulate silly, careless writing only if all other explanations fail.[15] It is clear that both chapters are directed against the same targets, present crimes against women as an index of social decadence, and employ similar rhetorical techniques.

Chapter 19 is marked by situational irony and promising beginnings that end in disaster. The travelers, having avoided the "foreign" Jerusalem, come to grief in an Israelite city. When the old Ephraimite invites the travelers in, hospitality seems to be restored—only to be breached in a far worse way. These techniques recur in chapter 21. The Israelites, apparently ruing their precipitous actions, speak of compassion and a fresh start. Yet are the Israelites really bewailing their misguided zeal in vv. 2–6? "Why has this happened in Israel?" is not "What have we done?" The impersonal construction (v. 3) and the passive (v. 6) are used to duck responsibility and to suggest that the events of the previous chapter simply happened. Why ask God a question to which you know the answer (v. 3)? In verse 15, the

---

12. This aspect, noted by the vast majority of scholars, is discussed in detail by Amit, "Literature in the Service of Politics"; *Hidden Polemics in Biblical Narrative,* 178–88.

13. Again, the majority of scholars take this view. A detailed exposition, covering the whole of Judges but focusing on 17–21, is O'Connell, *The Rhetoric of the Book of Judges.*

14. On this, see Exum, "Raped by the Pen," 177.

15. As Chesterton, *Varied Types,* 7, said of poets, they may be wrong in their metaphysics, but not in their prosody.

"breach in Israel" is put on YHWH's account. If this is not a quotation,[16] the author is guilty of atrocious theology.[17] In v. 16 matters are clear: "For the women have been exterminated from Benjamin." By whose hand, pray? An ironic reading suggests itself when the cure for one atrocity is the multiplication of atrocities of precisely the same kind. A flood of compassion for a "brother" and "a tribe in Israel" expresses itself in wiping out another "tribe" (cf. v. 5) of brothers. Is this the voice of compassion? "Women and children included. . . . This is what you must do to them—exterminate them!" (vv. 10–11). No careful author would insert such details and choose such constructions without reason.

Because irony by definition does not advertise itself,[18] a non-ironic reading of an ironic text is always possible. Here too the case for an ironic reading is not watertight: none of the positive indicators absolutely demands it. Still, the text is hardly readable in any other way. Can one imagine an author, a living human being, writing Judges 19–21 without ferocious irony? To posit such an author might nevertheless have existed would be pure speculation, speculation of a kind in which we should indulge only when no other options seem available.

IRONICALLY YOURS

Virtually all modern scholars[19] see the irony in Judges 19–21.[20] Irony, in spite of its indirect approach, is "readable," that is, we recognize it as an aspect of the human form of life. We may sometimes misread irony, assum-

16. Yielding the translation: The people had compassion with the Benjaminites, because "YHWH had made a breach in Israel." This much is suggested by Klein, *The Triumph of Irony*, 189, and Matthews, *Judges and Ruth*, 199.

17. But conceivably the pro-Davidic, pro-monarchic author also wants to discredit certain aspects of Israelite religion, cf. Boling, *Judges*, 293–94. Note that in chapter 20, the divine oracle, called in only after the vital decision had been taken, gives *pro forma* answers.

18. As Kierkegaard, *Concept of Irony*, 63, puts it, irony is "infinitely silent."

19. For a range of receptions of the text in former times, see Gunn, *Judges*, 231–72. Note, particularly, the ironic rendering of Gomersall in the seventeenth century, Gunn, *Judges*, 260–61.

20. Niditch, *Judges*, 11–13, 211, is exceptional in that she believes the author of these chapters retells old stories without moral comment, revealing perhaps "some embarrassment," but relishing them all the same. She recognizes irony in the story (192), but not an ironic author. Among those who strongly stress the ironic element are Lasine, "Guest and Host in Judges 19," and Klein, *Triumph of Irony*.

ing its presence when it is absent or *vice versa*, but we cannot imagine that we always do. Irony is "very human" and yet—or perhaps for that reason—somewhat mysterious. It presupposes an ability to read with and against the grain simultaneously, to see at once two points of view. In reading irony we differ from ourselves.

Generally, perhaps not invariably, our two selves are not equal. The self that understands the first sentence of *Pride and Prejudice*[21] as non-ironic earns the scorn of the self that adopts the ironic reading. Wayne Booth says: "If I am wrong about irony, I am wrong at deeper levels than I like to have exposed."[22] This observation indicates to what extent irony is entangled with ethics and shame. Kierkegaard points in the same direction when he says that irony springs from the discrepancy between what is and what should be.[23] Nevertheless, irony by itself is not an ethical category: it is neither a virtue nor a vice. The hierarchies that irony implicitly posits are not justified by the form of expression.

Therefore one cannot exempt Judges 21 from moral judgment by identifying it as an ironic narrative. Exum, speaking of Judges 19 in particular, sees the ironic twists, but nevertheless accuses the author of raping the concubine by the pen.[24] Though I do not entirely accept her arguments, I agree that irony invites further questioning. Irony posits hierarchies[25] and so does ethics (yes, it does!), but not all hierarchies are ethical and not all ethical discourse expresses itself in irony. I may, for factual or moral reasons, wish to negate or reverse the hierarchy that a particular ironist seeks to impose. This is not the case in Judges 21, where I recoil from the self that could see Israel's "solution" as remotely appropriate.[26] Therefore I accept that the author[27] portrayed the abominable treatment of women *because he regarded it as abominable*. The abomination makes his point.

---

21. "It is a truth universally acknowledged, that a single man in possession of a good fortune, must be in want of a wife," Austen, *Pride and Prejudice*, 11.

22. Booth, *Rhetoric of Irony*, 44.

23. Kierkegaard, *Concept of Irony*, 341.

24. Exum, "Raped by the Pen," 200–201.

25. As Booth, *Rhetoric of Irony*, 44, says, irony requires us "to construct alternative hierarchies and choose among them."

26. Remarkably, both Boling, "In Those Days"; *Judges*, 293, and Dumbrell, "In Those Days," believe that the ending is, in spite of everything, hopeful. Niditch, *Judges*, 211, also believes that the conclusion has the blessing of the narrator.

27. In speaking of an author here and elsewhere, I am not denying that Judges 19–21 had a complex literary history; I assume that there were *Vorstufen* and that the extant text

Only, this is not all that can or should be said. First, in saying, quite appropriately, "This should not be," the author merely hints at what should be—the Davidic monarchy. In view of 2 Samuel 13, one may question whether this changed anything. Rape and fratricide were not eliminated. Moreover, the irony works because the deck has been stacked—mercilessly if not *necessarily* unethically. Perhaps, just perhaps, all this was done in good faith. Then one may still ask several other questions, at least some of which involve ideology.

The shape of the text does not suggest that the author showed or assumed in the audience a callous disregard for women. On the contrary, crimes against women are portrayed to evoke outrage.[28] But this particular form of outrage is not only compatible with patriarchy, but may be a result of it. As Leith and Myerson have argued, women in distress "will always evoke powerful feelings as long as social relations continue to be based on patriarchy."[29] Chivalry is a product of patriarchy. That the author was probably counting on some form of chivalry among the audience does not make the author particularly chivalrous. Female characters are manipulated—not raped—by the pen, because they are "promising material" for an author who wishes to evoke shock and disgust.[30]

Often we forgive—or overlook such authorial manipulation, for all authors do, to some extent, "exploit" their characters. One cannot write fiction without doing so. Here, however, there are other factors. The violence in Judges 21, which strikes men and children too, is clearly and intentionally excessive: it borders on the pornography of violence.[31] The violence

---

was edited fairly extensively. Nor am I denying that the only author to whom we have access is the implied author. Mayes, *Deuteronomistic Royal Ideology*, 252–58, argues that we can also distinguish between the narrator and the implied author in these chapters. I doubt whether this is possible when it comes to an impersonal, third-person narrator.

28. The view that the author shows no concern for the concubine in chapter 19 (see, for instance, Trible, *Texts of Terror*, 76; Exum, "Raped by the Pen," 182, 197) is untenable from a literary perspective. The precise wording of vv. 25–28 did not descend from heaven, nor is it a necessity imposed by the plot. Niditch, *Judges*, 193, rightly says that the scene is filled with pathos, and Keefe, "Rapes of Women," 91, that it heightens "the reader's empathy for the tortured woman." If one acknowledges that Judges 19–21 directs by indirection and consistently says "This should not be," the only possible conclusion is the one drawn by Keefe: maltreatment of women is regarded as a sign of social chaos.

29. Leith and Myerson, *Power of Address*, 61.

30. Thus I maintain that the view expounded by Keefe in "Rapes of Women" does more justice to the literary shape of the text than that of Exum, "Raped by the Pen".

31. Not even chapter 19 can be compared to "ordinary pornography" (*pace* Exum,

has a *general* dehumanizing effect, which, if anything, touches the female characters less than the male ones. Whereas the women of Jabesh and Shiloh evoke sympathy and are humanized by it, the Israelite (and partly the Benjaminite) men appear barely human. "Their version of the story" is practically unreadable by itself and lives only through its ironic obverse.

I grant willingly that authors often need villains, even repulsive ones. I may grant also—without fully believing it—that how authors treat their fictional characters is not a moral matter. Even so, one has to ask how one can immerse oneself in horror, writing with relentless ironic negativity unmitigated by any overtly positive features, and emerge unscathed. Kenneth Burke[32] warns that "a purely admonitory idiom," because it creates "nothing but the image of the enemy," may fail in its deterrent purpose. In representing only the bad, it offers nothing but the bad for us to identify with. The same goes for irony. The ironic representation assumes a strong balancing positivity on the part of both the author and the reader: it affirms by denying. Yet how long can the balance be maintained if the positive is not given determinate presence? Irony is a trope of human mastery, but the dangers that we shall be mastered by our trope cannot be discounted. If this is not exactly criticism of the author of Judges 19–21, it is cause for serious reservations.

IT TAKES ONE TO KNOW ONE

I have presumed to sit in judgment on an author—not a text, an economy of textuality, an ideological construct, or a discursive formation. This is always a morally hazardous enterprise and never more so than when the evidence is a text replete with interpretive difficulties. I had to assume that the text is not *simply* indeterminate: the weight of evidence suggests that it is bitterly ironic, driven by a specific rhetorical intention, and written with subtle mastery of rhetorical strategies. It is shocking because it intends to shock.

To humanize the author (for moral judgments pertains to moral agents), I had to assume a human face. A judge is not the "brief elaboration of a law," and may not, if the judgment is to be moral, plead that a particular theory enforces a mandatory sentence. Since judges are as fallible as those who appear before them, justice has since time immemorial required judges to hear the other party. In pronouncing a verdict, judges seem godlike; in

---

"Raped by the Pen," 196–99).

32. Burke, *Grammar of Motives,* 331–32.

listening carefully, they are members of the human family, entangled in the endless human conversation and open, therefore, to conversion. The judicial monologue, the interminable drone of theory, has to yield to a dialogue in which the dock and the bench are in principle interchangeable.

First one has to review the "*prima facie* evidence" by reading the text without prematurely forcing the evidence into a theoretical Procrustean bed. The accused has a long record and must be guilty; the text is from a patriarchal society and has to be hostile to women. Nor should judges be swayed by a single bit of suggestive evidence. Because the accused's fingerprints were found on the scene, the accused committed the murder; because one or two verses, conceivably glosses, point in one direction, the rest of the text must bear the same stamp. Self-evident really, but frequently forgotten when scholarly judges forget their humanity and speak in the name of infallible theory.

Perhaps we may and sometimes should go further than that. Having established that a killing took place, a judge has to decide whether this was murder, culpable homicide, or justifiable self-defense. Then the evidence of the accused is needed to contextualize the factual evidence.[33] Although we cannot summon biblical authors to testify, we can to an extent award them a voice. If we can read irony, which implies the ability to hold more than one position simultaneously, we may construct possible replies and evaluate their plausibility. What could the author of Judges 19–21, endowed with sufficient knowledge of our context, say to us?

> Because I took sides in a political dispute for money, you call me a lackey, yet your committed academics do the same on public funding. I call myself an activist who, without illusions about Davidic rule, chose what seemed the lesser evil. Some of your scholars and moralists defended Hitler, Stalin, and Mao for similar reasons. My case had to be and was plausible. Tenured academics like the idea of anarchy; in our poor society anarchy worked for the robber barons, not the weak. I hear that it is still so—in your slums. So I spoke for strong central government, not unrepresentative tribal leadership, just as you do when your fears overcome you.
>
> Surely you noticed that I implicitly spoke for the weak? While violence against women was as common in our society as

33. I have to object to the procedure of those critics who, in the name of contextual criticism, point out how a particular biblical text, read (rather badly) in a particular context may have negative effects. They demand, effectively, that biblical texts propound decontextualized truths so that contextualized audiences should not be misled. And if they are simply saying that fire is both useful and dangerous, why do they bother?

it is in yours, most of us regarded it as despicable, as no doubt most of you do. That is why I wrote as I did. Even if we differ on how the dignity of women is best served, we may agree that they should suffer no sexual and physical abuse. Yes, I "manipulated" my female characters by making them victims—which is what they often were. I was more unfair to my male characters by making them, almost without exception, villains. The majority were not as black as I had painted them.

Arguably I overindulged in violence, but the literature of your less violent society is no whit less violent. Does the charge of "pornography of violence" hold against Tarentino films and violent video games? In trying to do a thorough job, I pulled out all the stops and cried "Havoc" so diabolically efficiently that I sometimes neglected to be human or to humanize my characters. As one of your authors said, being human implies being "rotten with perfection."[34] Still, genuine concern may be voiced with bitter ferocity, though you run the risk of becoming like your enemy. The misunderstood, embittered author of *A Modest Proposal* is a case in point.[35] I won't say more about my motives, because it is all too easy to fool yourself.

You say my text has a particularly bad effect because it is in the Bible. I don't get what this has to do with me. I wasn't writing the Bible and I hardly know what the Bible is.

"Unfair!" cries the jury, "The judge testified for the accused."

Consider please that all judges necessarily do this unless they are content to pronounce sentence uncritically. They have to rehearse in their minds the case for the defense and that for the prosecution and weigh the two.[36]

Here I constructed from scant evidence one plausible defense without making great claims for it. My intention was not to establish facts, but to conjure up a human face, to show how hard it is to say "case closed" in facing a human face. Having expressed some skepticism about the indeterminacy of texts, I wish to express even graver doubts about the determining effect of ideology (and its hypostases), about its ability to efface the human

34. See Burke, *Language as Symbolic Action,* 16.

35. In *A Modest Proposal* (1729), Jonathan Swift suggested that most of the many children of poor Irish families should be sold to the rich as food, thereby lessening the burden on the parents and benefitting the public. Some took this as a serious proposal and even those who did not deplored the ferocity of the writing. See Price, *The Restoration,* 221–27.

36. Eagleton, *Ideology,* 171–72, rightly appeals to the Marxist notion of immanent critique, without adding that all critical judgments (as opposed to unconsidered reactions) contain an element of immanent critique.

face. And when the human face appears, because it is a human face and not a version to be subverted, we have to assume human faces ourselves. When I listen to the plea of the human author, no matter how inadequate and pathetic it is, I myself become questionable, accountable, responsible—perhaps even more so when the plea is pathetic indeed.

THE DIALECTIC OF DIGNITY AND SHAME

In reading irony, we hold two views at once, balancing their claims on us, just as we do in judging. In misreading irony, we lose our grip and put ourselves in the balance. Having read the first sentence in *Pride and Prejudice* with an assenting nod, I cannot blithely revise my previous reading when I find the sentence was intended ironically. I am ashamed, for I have exposed myself to the scorn of an author whom I had hailed as a fellow soul. I cannot simply return the scorn if Jane Austen's voice is otherwise compelling: I may wish to have her as a fellow soul, not as a harsh judge.

The pain of shame does not derive solely from social disapproval, which I sometimes ignore when I do not feel that I also stand condemned in my own eyes, by my own principles.[37] When Heidegger became a Nazi, he incurred, by common consent, guilt. How much guilt is not for me to say. Perhaps he resolutely chose what he saw as a lesser evil, a movement that could in time shed its dubious elements.[38] When he allowed the dedication to Husserl to be removed from the fifth edition (1941) of *Sein und Zeit,* he did nothing momentous, for Husserl was no longer alive.[39] But could he look back on this act, which can by no stretch of the imagination be called "resolute," without shame? It would cause me shame to think that he could, just as I found a non-ironic reading of Judges 21 shameful. I am not resolute enough to imagine either Heidegger or an anonymous author so bereft of dignity as to be unable to feel shame.

For shame (not indignity *per se*) is the *alter ego* of human dignity; it is the shadow cast where the sun of dignity shines. Just as I may be misguided in my assertions of and feelings about human dignity, so I may be about shame. Though shame is not an infallible moral compass, which is not what

37. See Slenczka, "To Be Ashamed," 259–60; the entire article is relevant to this section.

38. On this, see Inwood, *Heidegger,* 117–18.

39. He claimed that this was done at the request of the publisher; see Inwood, *Dictionary,* 28.

Bonhoeffer had in mind when he argued that shame is more fundamental than remorse,[40] shame cannot easily be explained as a social construct.[41] The moment of shame marks the place where two simultaneously held views can no longer be ironized and where my judgments, if I still feel able to make them, touch me directly. In shame I lose the distance of irony and the self-assurance of the moral judge.

For all that, shame is not purely private. Indeed, it is "before the face of X" that I feel ashamed, even when I am alone.[42] I could call X "my own better self," but in feeling shame I feel that I have lost touch with that better self.[43] Thus I cannot simply judge myself (as I can when I feel guilty), because at that moment I have no access to the bench. My *alter ego*, the version of myself that has dignity, is externalized and confronts me with the face of the other—or the Other. There is no firmer confirmation of human dignity than the one that issues from shame. Disgraced and unable to assert my purely personal dignity, I beg for affirmation of that dignity that pertains to me as human. Unable to face myself and award myself a dignified office, I need other faces to assure me that the regal still belongs to the human. When I have lost access to the version of myself that I can affirm, I need restoration, not subversion; I wish to be reverted, but I look to others for that.

We may also reverse (not subvert) the picture. When we, as judges or as ironists, come to the defense of human dignity, what exactly are we doing? Having shown solidarity with the victims, assuring them that they have not been effaced, but still face us as equals, what do we do what about the perpetrators? If we beat them down by sword or pen and subvert their (racist, sexist, elitist) versions, we become versions of them. If we simply judge them, they may reply, "That is your justice, not ours"—and beat us down. In the interest of human dignity, we have to award them faces, not

40. Bonhoeffer, *Ethics*, 6.

41. Though shame gets its determinate shape through social construction, here, as often elsewhere, the social construction argument runs out of steam and becomes circular if pressed. Social approval and disapproval often determine *what* evokes shame in a particular person; it does not explain why specifically shame is evoked. In the absence of other sanctions, people often enough thumb their noses at social disapproval. The argument that social disapproval is associated with further sanctions does not work either. This association may cause feelings of apprehension, fear, or even guilt. Shame seems to be relatively independent of these feelings. My guess is that explanations of this kind ultimately smuggle the *definiendum* (or its dialectical opposite) into the definition.

42. See Slenczka, "To Be Ashamed," 262–63.

43. As Slenczka puts it, shame ruptures my "friendship with myself" (ibid., 260).

categorize them under ideological rubrics, speak to and of their unique dignity, not deny their humanity.[44] If those we criticize are not human and dignified enough to feel shame, our only tools are violence and fear. By these we may tame, that is, dehumanize, them … having surreptitiously abandoned the notion of human dignity.

Irony is a trope of mastery and judging an act of power. They belong in their different ways to what I call human queenship rather than human dignity. In irony and in judging we juggle perspectives, sometimes merrily, sometimes in great earnest, from a relatively secure *locus standi*. In shame we have lost our footing; we can neither subvert nor revert. That is when we most need others, others with sufficient queenly dignity, to restore us. That is when we need restorative readings.

RESTORING THE HUMAN TO DIGNITY

Restorative readings cannot restore human dignity if we randomly impose them on texts, or if they are deterministically imposed on us by our ideologies or interpretive communities. When we read ancient texts, much indeed remains "ultimately undecidable"; when we read any texts, the influence of our multi-layered contexts is indeed never absent. Yet we still pride ourselves on reading critically, which presupposes that we are not reproducing prefabricated ideological constructs or constructing judgments without textual constraints.

We also continue to read irony as irony, which presupposes that texts are not merely methodological fields awaiting our creative activity. As Booth points out, reconstructing the meaning of irony depends on "your hunches about my hunches about your hunches."[45] Irony cannot be pinned down formally; to identify irony is to identify a human voice, a human mind and human intentions.[46] It is this human aspect, not aspects of textu-

---

44. As Timothy Snyder, *Bloodlands*, 320, points out, in 1945 Edvard Beneš publicly said that the German nation "had ceased to be human." Already in 1942, Ilya Ehrenburg (as a Jew) had written: "From now on, we have to understand that the Germans are not humans," Snyder, *Bloodlands*, 317. Needless to say, tens of thousands of noncombatant Germans died—those who were not murdered in labor camps or as a result of brutal "ethnic cleansing"—and countless German women were raped, often many times, towards the end of the war and immediately thereafter; see Snyder, *Bloodlands*, 313–27. Judges 20–21 does not belong to the past.

45. Booth, "Pleasures and Perils," 6.

46. Which is why Booth, "Pleasures and Perils," 10, says that he cannot explain irony

ality that is open to our *moral* judgments,[47] though the relationship, being human, is reciprocal. After all, the ironist also imposed a moral judgment: judging and writing ironically are analogous operations.

This opens the critical scholar to the critical gaze of the ironic author, for we can be painfully and shamefully mistaken in judging and identifying irony. Our mutual critical appraisals are terminated when one of the parties adopt the appraisal of the other in shame. Shame, which Slenczka calls negative self-awareness,[48] is indeed *self*-awareness, but it is mediated through the perspective of the other. It is loss of dignity, but any substantive conception of dignity presupposes the possibility of shame. Shame, like irony, works through negation, but in shame the irony is turned against us so that the judging roles are reversed, often because the judge has not adequately considered the other side of the case.

Perhaps we can look at the events of Judges 19–21 without feeling guilty;[49] I cannot imagine looking at them without feeling *ashamed*. The intentions—ideology, if you like—of the author are recognized by most scholars. What this author wrote from a particular context we judge, not necessarily unfairly, from another context.[50] We may also judge the means employed by the author to convey these intentions, as I suggested above. But exactly here, regarding those strategies that the author chose to give fitting, but not uniquely fitting, shape to an argument, the case may slip from our control. We may be overtaken, not by the awareness of our no doubt

---

"without referring to probabilities about the intentions of real authors."

47. When Exum, "Raped by the Pen," 191, says of Judges 19 that "the text criticizes its own ideology," she is at best using a somewhat misleading shorthand. Certainly, a text written by a single author may contain several voices and that these may be at odds with one another, because we are not "centered subjects." Thus I find that Alice Bach, "Rereading the Body Politic," speaks in two voices: a compelling voice insisting on personalization and a voice that depersonalizes in accordance with theory. Instead of asking which ideology is criticizing which, I shall assume that the second voice derives from fashion.

48. Slenczka, "To Be Ashamed," 257.

49. Thus Exum, "Raped by the Pen," 197.

50. Brettler, *Judges*, 11–21, provides a balanced discussion of the rival claims of synchronic and diachronic readings, noting that some literary readings elide the context in a misleading way. I cannot discuss the vexed question of the context of Judges 19–21 here, but I find the context proposed by Yee, "Ideological Criticism," 158–67, more plausible than the one proposed by Guillaume, *Waiting for Josiah*, 198–226. The point here is that if criticism directed from one context to someone in another context is invalid, all criticism is invalid.

laudable motives and our no doubt ineluctable contexts, but by the negative self-awareness that we could have read and judged differently.

Offences against human dignity abound in Judges 19–21. Have we located the evil, perhaps, as the Israelites did, without questioning the Levite's story too carefully, without asking too many questions about guilt and innocence?[51] Or should we show solidarity, as indiscriminately as the Benjaminites did, with some group of sisters or brothers? To the barricades! And then, when we have wreaked disproportionate revenge by sword or pen, do we theorize, with copious tears, the breaches that have "appeared," ascetically denying ourselves agency? Time for running repairs: either a new culprit can be found or some morally dubious fancy footwork will get us off the hook. And so the carnage continues.

Theoretically dismembering the human body by calling it a text composed of disseminated signs will not restore it to dignity. Nor will it help to bewail the collateral damage when each person inevitably does what is right in the eyes of her or his interpretive community (or ideological determinants). To get a restorative reading from Judges 19–21 one has to "subvert" it, to show its obverse. It does not distort the text, for this is how one reads irony. To restore the human being to dignity, one has to restore the "human" to our conception of dignity, also in the reading of texts. Whenever I try to do this—no doubt ineffectually—I find that I am a royalist (not a monarchist) after all, because I want queenship for all human beings. And then, recalling some sons and daughters of Belial that I know, I add *sotto voce*: "Of course, the right *kind* of queenship".[52]

BIBLIOGRAPHY

Amit, Yairah. *Hidden Polemics in Biblical Narrative*. Translated by J. Chapman. Biblical Interpretation Series 25. Leiden: Brill, 2000.

———. "Literature in the Service of Politics: Studies in Judges 19–21." In *Politics and Theopolitics in the Bible and Postbiblical Literature*, edited by Henning G. Reventlow, Yair Hoffman, and Benjamin Uffenheimer, 28–40. JSOTSup 171. Sheffield, UK: JSOT, 1994.

51. "The congregation of . . . Israel questions the accuser but makes no effort to hear the accused," Klein, *Triumph of Irony*, 177. As Jones-Warsaw, "Toward a Womanist Hermeneutic," 25–26, points out, none of the victims in Judges 19–21 is given a voice. See also Keefe, "Rapes of Women," 92.

52. This corresponds to Satterthwaite's conclusion that the narrative is pro-monarchic in a qualified way: "[N]ot any king will do . . . ," "No King in Israel," 88.

Appiah, Kwame Anthony. "Tolerable Falsehoods: Agency and the Interests of Theory." In *Consequences of Theory*, edited by J. Arac and B. Johnson, 63–90. Baltimore: Johns Hopkins University Press, 1991.

Austen, Jane. *Pride and Prejudice*. New York: Middleton Classics, 2009.

Bach, Alice. "Rereading the Body Politic: Women and Violence in Judges 21." *Biblical Interpretation* 6/1 (1998) 1–19.

Bal, Mieke. "Between Altar and Wandering Rock: Toward a Feminist Philology." In *Anti-Covenant: Counter-Reading Women's Lives in the Hebrew Bible*, edited by Mieke Bal, 211–31. Sheffield, UK: Almond, 1989.

Barthes, Roland. "The Death of the Author." In *Image, Music, Text*. Selected and translated by Stephen Heath, 142–48. London: Fontana, 1977.

Becker, Uwe. *Richterzeit und Königtum: Redaktionsgeschichtliche Studien zum Richterbuch.* BZAW 192. Berlin: De Gruyter, 1990.

Boling, Robert G. "'In Those Days There Was No King in Israel.'" In *A Light unto my Path: Old Testament Studies in Honor of J. M. Myers*, edited by Howard N. Bream, Ralph D. Heim, and Carey A. Moore, 33–48. Philadelphia: Fortress, 1974.

———. *Judges*. AB 6A. Garden City, NY: Doubleday, 1975.

Bonhoeffer, Dietrich. *Ethics*. Translated by N. H. Smith. London: SCM, 1964.

Booth, Wayne C. "The Pleasures and Pitfalls of Irony: Or, Why Don't You Say What You Mean?" In *Rhetoric, Philosophy, and Literature*, edited by Don M. Burks, 1–13. West Lafayette: Purdue University Press, 1978.

———. *A Rhetoric of Irony*. Chicago: University of Chicago Press, 1974.

Brettler, Marc Zvi. *The Book of Judges*. Old Testament Readings. London: Routledge, 2002.

Burke, Kenneth D. *A Grammar of Motives*. New York: Prentice-Hall, 1952.

———. *Language as Symbolic Action: Essays on Life, Literature, and Method*. Berkeley: University of California Press, 1966.

Butler, Christopher. "The Future of Reading: Saving the Reader." In *The Future of Literary Theory*, edited by R. Cohen, 229–49. London: Routledge, 1989.

Chesterton, Gilbert Keith. *Varied Types*. New York: Dodd, Mead and Company, 1903.

Crüsemann, Frank. *Der Widerstand gegen das Königtum: Die antiköniglichen Texte des Alten Testaments und das Kampf um den frühen Israelitischen Staat*. WMANT 49. Neukirchen: Neukirchener Verlag, 1978.

Davies, Eryl. *The Dissenting Reader: Feminist Approaches to the Hebrew Bible*. Aldershot, UK: Ashgate, 2003.

Dumbrell, William J. "'In Those Days There Was No King in Israel; Every Man Did What Was Right in his Own Eyes.' The Purpose of the Book Judges Reconsidered." *JSOT* 25 (1983) 23–33.

Eagleton, Terry. *Ideology: An Introduction*. London: Verso, 1991.

Exum, J. Cheryl. "Raped by the Pen." In *Fragmented Women: Feminist (Sub)versions of Biblical Narratives*, 170–201. JSOTSup 163. Sheffield, UK: JSOT, 1993.

Eynikel, Erik. "Judges 19–21, an 'Appendix': Rape, Murder, War and Abduction." *Communio Viatorum* 47/2 (2005) 101–15.

Guillaume, Phillippe. *Waiting for Josiah: The Judges*. JSOTSup 385. London: T. & T. Clark, 2004.

Gunn, David M. *Judges*. Blackwell Bible Commentaries. London: Blackwell, 2005.

Hume, David. *A Treatise of Human Nature*, edited by E. G. Mossner. Harmondsworth, UK: Penguin, 1969.

Inwood, Michael. *Heidegger*. Past Masters. Oxford: Oxford University Press, 1997.

———. *A Heidegger Dictionary*. Oxford: Blackwell, 1999.

Jones-Warsaw, Koala. "Toward a Womanist Hermeneutic: A Reading of Judges 19–21." In *A Feminist Companion to Judges*, edited by Athalya Brenner, 172–86. Sheffield, UK: Sheffield Academic Press, 1993.

Jüngling, Hans-Winfried. *Richter 19—Ein Plädoyer für das Königtum*. Analecta Biblica 84. Rome: Biblical Institute, 1981.

Kamuf, Peggy. "Author of a Crime." In *A Feminist Companion to Judges*, edited by Athalya Brenner, 187–207. Sheffield, UK: Sheffield Academic Press, 1993.

Keefe, Alice A. "Rapes of Women/Wars of Men." *Semeia* 61 (1993) 79–97.

Kierkegaard, Søren. *The Concept of Irony*. Translated by L. M. Capel. London: Collins, 1966.

Klein, Lillian R. *The Triumph of Irony in the Book of Judges*. JSOTSup 68. Sheffield, UK: Almond, 1988.

Lasine, Stuart. "Guest and Host in Judges 19: Lot's Hospitality in an Inverted World." *JSOT* 29 (1984) 37–59.

Leith, Dick and George Myerson. *The Power of Address: Explorations in Rhetoric*. London: Routledge, 1989.

Matthews, Victor H. *Judges and Ruth*. New Cambridge Bible Commentary. Cambridge: Cambridge University Press, 2004.

Mayes, Andrew D. H. "Deuteronomistic Royal Ideology in Judges 17–21." *Biblical Interpretation* 9/3 (2001) 241–58.

Niditch, Susan. *Judges*. OTL. Louisville, KY: Westminster John Knox, 2008.

O'Connell, Robert H. *The Rhetoric of the Book of Judges*. SVT 63. Leiden: Brill, 1996.

Price, Martin. *The Restoration and Eighteenth Century*. The Oxford Anthology of English Literature. Oxford: Oxford University Press, 1973.

Satterthwaite, Philip E. "'No King in Israel': Narrative Criticism and Judges 19–21." *Tyndale Bulletin* 44/1 (1993) 75–88.

Slenczka, Notger. "'To Be Ashamed': On the Meaning and Fruit of a Phenomenology of Negative Self-Awareness." *NGTT* 51/3 (2010) 257–65.

Snyder, Timothy. *Bloodlands: Europe between Hitler and Stalin*. London: Vintage, 2011.

Tompkins, Jane P. "An Introduction to Reader-Response Criticism." In *Reader-Response Criticism: From Formalism to Post-Structuralism*, edited by J. P. Tompkins, ix–xxvi. Baltimore: Johns Hopkins University Press, 1980.

Trible, Phyllis. *Texts of Terror: Literary-feminist Readings of Biblical Narratives*. Overtures to Biblical Theology Series 13. Philadelphia: Fortress, 1984.

Yee, Gale A. "Ideological Criticism: Judges 17–21 and the Dismembered Body." In *Judges and Method: New Approaches in Biblical Studies*, edited by G. A. Yee, 146–70. Minneapolis: Fortress, 1995.

PART 3

Injustice

4

"It's the Price I Guess for the Lies I've Told that the Truth it No Longer Thrills Me . . .":

Reading Queer Lies to Reveal Straight Truth in Genesis 38

Charlene van der Walt,

Faculty of Theology, Stellenbosch University

INTRODUCTION

THE CLASSIC DICTUM READS that a life unexamined is not worth living. Reflecting ethically on one's situatedness is, however, no simple task. Hard and fast rules that apply to every situation are impossible to come by. This fact rings especially true for those whose lived realities do not strictly conform to the dominant expectation. Queer people in a heteronormative society are often compelled to trick and lie in order to survive. Unfortunately, the price paid for the lies told can often lead to a truth that is less than thrilling, that is life-denying. In an attempt to find a creative alternative to dominantly constructed rules regarding morality, I turn to the genre of narrative. Stanley Hauerwas points to the potential alternative space for modern ethical reflection when remarking:

> Christians do not have a "morality" per se, but rather our morality is embedded in the stories that require constant retellings. Telling a story, particularly stories like those Christians tell of God's dealings with them, is a frightening business since in the telling one frequently has the story retold in a manner that is surprising and challenging to the teller.[1]

According to Hauerwas, it is in the telling and retelling of the stories of faith that we learn who we are as a faith community, but also what is expected of us and how to live an ethical life. Denise Ackermann continues along the same lines when stating:

> Telling stories is intrinsic to claiming one's identity and in the process finding impulses for hope. Narrative has a further function. Apart from claiming identity and naming the evil, narrative has a sense-making function. The very act of telling the story is an act of making sense of an often incomprehensible situation, of a suffering and chaotic world in which people wrestle with understanding and in so doing seek to experience relief.[2]

This essay aims to employ the strategy suggested by Hauerwas when the telling and retelling of stories of faith as captured in biblical narratives become a reflective surface[3] for ethical reflection by contemporary readers. In deducing ethical pointers from biblical narratives, I take my cue from the work of Jacqueline Lapsley who states:

> For the most part I want to move away from asking which characters are worth emulating or not, and which text is "good" or "bad." As a rule, the kind of ethical reflection I propose here asks the reader to allow herself to be drawn into a complex moral world evoked by the narrative. In the narrative worlds of the Old Testament easy moral judgments are elusive and most often miss the

1. Hauerwas, *Christians in the Hands*, 32.

2. Ackermann, *Tamar's Cry*, 18–19.

3. Within the process of contextual Bible reading, complex biblical narratives are often used as a so-called "reflective surface." The text becomes the point of reference in a conversation where the singular reader as constructed in the traditional bipolar model of biblical interpretation is replaced by a more realistic diversity of readers around the biblical text in a multipolar model. Rainer Kessler describes this conceptual shift in "From Bipolar to Multipolar Understanding," 452–59.

mark. The kind of ethics I envision has more to do with how the reader enters into the story—it is narrative ethics—and less to do with the reading standing outside the story making ethical judgments about character.[4]

It is important to note that Lapsley's understanding of narrative ethics is rooted in the emotional response of the reader to the text and the reader's capacity to empathize with the characters in the story. It is with this point of departure in mind that I approach the story of Tamar in Genesis 38 in which we meet a well-known trickster, one who maneuvered herself out of a tight spot and who resisted ultimate identity definitions in the process of employing concealment in order to reveal the truth. Ultimately the reading that follows is based upon the belief that Tamar's story is one that has the potential to resonate with those who have found themselves powerless and voiceless and who has continued to search for life-affirming alternatives to the so-called dominant truth.

QUEER IDENTITY IN A HETERONORMATIVE SOCIETY

Being "straight" in a heteronormative society requires no explanation, for being a man who longs for a life-fulfilling union with a woman is self-explanatory. There is no need for discussion or evaluations of the longing to share one's life with a significant other. No interrogation of values or ethics is needed if one expresses the desire to be with someone, to create a life together, and to negotiate the complexities of everyday life with a partner, as long as the union conforms to the heterosexual norm. No one raises an eyebrow at the wish to get married, buy a house, have children and find a job (whether in ministry or teaching) as long as the wish implies the heterosexual other. All the above-mentioned longings and desires are normal, for being heterosexual in a heteronormative society is normal.

Heteronormativity is the result of a systematic normalization of heterosexuality. Gust Yep describes this process as follows: "The process of normalization of heterosexuality in our social system actively and methodically subordinates, disempowers, denies, and rejects individuals who do not conform to the heterosexual mandate by criminalizing them, denying

4. Lapsley, *Whispering the Word*, 11.

them protection against discrimination, refusing them basic rights and recognition, or all of the above."[5]

Heteronormative discourse describes reality primarily and exclusively from the position of the heterosexual. According to Andrew Martin, "this is the idea, dominant in most societies, that heterosexuality is the only 'normal' sexual orientation, only sexual or marital relations between women and men are acceptable and each sex has certain natural roles in life, so-called gender roles."[6] Within the heteronormative, there is only space for heterosexual experiences, constructions and realities and no other alternatives are tolerated. Heteronormativity often gives rise to homophobic attitudes and hate crimes.[7]

Within the African context, heteronormativity is reinforced by describing homosexuality as un-African, un-Christian, and counter to the biblical norm. Lovemore Togarasei and Ezra Chitando clearly illuminate the sources of the so-called un-African argument against homosexuality which contends that the whole debate on same-sex sexuality is in fact part of the Western agenda of cultural imperialism which has adopted a false reading of human rights when they point to two categories of African intellectuals: "In the first instance one could identify African intellectuals who wield political power. A number of African male presidents have used the cultural thesis to oppose same-sex sexuality.[8] The second category of African intellectuals that has appropriated culture in the discourse on homo-

---

5. Yep et al., *Queer Theory and Communication*, 24.

6. Martin et al., *Hate Crimes*, 1.

7. South Africa is also considered to be the birthplace of so-called "'corrective rape': an act of violence against women committed by men ostensibly to 'cure' lesbians of their nonconforming sexual orientation—or correct it—the belief being that homosexuality is an imported white disease (from the colonial empire)." Di Silvio, "Correcting Corrective Rape," 1469. It is especially "African women and girls thought to be lesbian that become victims of corrective rape, with the claimed purpose of turning them into 'real African women,'" Kelly, in De Silvio, "Correcting Corrective Rape," 1470. "Attackers, often family members, friends, or neighbors of the victims, say they are teaching lesbian women 'a lesson' by raping them and 'showing them how to be "a real woman,"'" Di Silvio 1471–72. Although black lesbians are the main targets of corrective rape, any woman with a nonconforming sexual identity is at risk, seeing that the aim or goal is to "cure" or simply to punish any nonconforming sexual orientations. Thus, any woman thought to be "too different" or "insufficiently feminine" and who "fails to stay invisible" is at risk. "Accordingly 86% of black lesbians from the Western Cape said they lived in fear of sexual assault," Di Silvio, 1471.

8. Togarasei and Chitando here refer to Robert Mugabe of Zimbabwe, Yoweri Museveni of Uganda, and the previous president of Namibia, Sam Nujoma.

sexuality consists of certain church leaders and theologians."[9] The so-called "un-African" arguments against homosexuality fail to observe that "African culture" is in itself a contested term. There is no consensus on what "African culture" means as it consists of a diversity of lived experiences; it is never static, but rather a dynamic developing notion. To be truly African means to take seriously diversity, as Robin Petersen states:

> Resistance to this universalizing and imperialist tendency, there-fore, means an assertion of the radically, irreducibly plural nature of human existence. It implies a fundamental respect for the Other, one that does not and will not attempt to reduce the Other to the Same. Life is basically dialogical, like a good conversation. It is a relationship that retains its distance; it is a face-to-face engage-ment that respects the "otherness of the other"; it is committed to hearing the voice of the Other. Pluralism, thus, is a given fact of political, cultural, theological and religious life.[10]

"Un-African" arguments also fail to contend with numerous stories and examples of same-sex individuals and communities within the African collective.

Within faith communities, heteronormative perceptions of masculin-ity and homophobic attitudes among communities are clearly formed by religious beliefs and fueled by conservative religious leaders. These notions are often formed by exclusivist practices of Bible interpretation. Choon-Leong Seow divides texts used against the practice of homosexuality into four categories: Legal texts that explicitly forbid same-sex relationships (Lev 18:22 and 20:13); narrative passages that are said to illustrate its wrongful-ness (Gen 19:1–14 and Judg 19:22); New Testament lists of inappropriate and wrongful behavior (Rom 1:26–27; 1 Cor 6:9–10; 1 Tim 1:9–10); and the creation accounts in Genesis 1–2.[11] Fundamentalist, exclusivist, uncriti-cal and non-contextual reading of the above-mentioned texts has become the foundational basis for communities and societies that perpetuate vio-lence against gay people and the construction of exclusivist communities where homophobia is rife.

Critical voices have challenged faith communities to oppose discrimi-nation and homophobia. Nobel prize winner Archbishop Desmond Tutu condemned in no uncertain terms the negative stance which churches have

---

9. Togarasei and Chitando, *Beyond the Bible*, 114–23.

10. Petersen, "Theological and Religious Pluralism," 223.

11. Seow, "Textual Orientation," 17–34.

taken in relation to gay and lesbian individuals. He states, "I have found the position of the church illogical, irrational and frankly un-Christian, totally untenable," and he continues that "if the church, after the victory of apartheid, is looking for a worthy moral crusade, then this is it: the fight against homophobia and heterosexism."[12]

However limiting and exclusivist, heteronormativity and its resulting normative assumptions are an undeniable modern cultural reality. As Virginia Mollenkott argues: "In a heteropatriarchal culture, like our own, queer people are distinctly 'other' and distinctly secondary, forced to compete uphill on a slanted playing field."[13] Being other than the norm, being queer, implies/demands explanations, redefinition and ultimately moments of self-revelation. Being queer implies "coming out," and "coming out" is complicated. "Coming out" can be defined as the process of acknowledging one's sexual orientation to oneself and/or others and the development of an alternative gender identity.[14] It is a process that never ends, as every new friendship or social space implies yet again the stating of identity.

I choose to use the term "queer," rather than one of the more stable identity markers such as lesbian, gay, transgender, bisexual, or intersex, because I deliberately want to make space for those "allies" who identify as being straight but have some sort of political empathy with the plight of those who are outside the norm.[15] "Queer" creates space for all those who want to "que(e)ry" or have trouble or make trouble within the confines of the heteronormative norm.[16]

12. Tutu, "Foreword," no page.

13. Mollenkott, "Reading the Bible," 19.

14. Jordan and Deluty, "Coming Out for Lesbian Women", 42.

15. Cheng, *Radical Love*, 3 alludes to the term "queer" as an umbrella term when stating: "One common use of the word 'queer' is as an umbrella term that refers collectively to lesbian, gay, bisexual, transgender, intersex, questioning, and other individuals who identify with non-normative sexualities and/or gender identities. The term 'queer' also can include 'allies' who may not themselves identify as lesbian, gay, bisexual, transgender, intersex or questioning, but stand in solidarity with their queer sisters and brothers in terms of seeking a more just world with respect to sexuality and gender identity. In other words, 'queer' is a synonym for acronyms such as LGBTIQA."

16. Schneider, "Queer Theory," 206, describes the task of queer theory: "In general, queer theory seeks to disrupt modernist notions of fixed sexuality and gender ... by appropriating post-structuralist critiques of 'natural' identities.... Queer theory 'queers' taken-for-granted cultural associations concerning all sexual identities (and the social placements that adhere to those identities) by revealing the vulnerability of history and politics and therefore, to change."

As a result of my inclusive choice for the term "queer," the definition of "coming out" expands to include the actions of solidarity by those who choose to stand on the side of the minority and by those who speak on behalf of the marginalized—those who "speak out." I am thus using the term in a broader sense, not only referring exclusively to the process of identity negotiation by LGTBI individuals, but also the risky business of standing on the side of the marginalized and the disenfranchised. Although numerous examples can be quoted to show the complexity (and danger) of the above-mentioned process, I will limit myself to two examples.

Church Leaders in Africa–Speaking about "Speaking Out"

I recently had the opportunity to attend a meeting of African Anglicans and American Episcopalians who met to discuss sexuality and Scripture at the Jumuia Conference Centre in Limuru, Kenya.[17] The meeting was convened by the Chicago Consultation and the Ujamaa Centre of the University of Kwa-Zulu Natal in Pietermaritzburg, South Africa. The group of twenty-seven African Anglicans, sixteen Episcopalians and several ecumenical friends gathered in order to explore issues of sexuality in dialogue with Scripture. The framework of the consultation—a liberation theology methodology called "See, Judge, Act"—encouraged participants to listen to the experience of those who are marginalized due to their sexuality and read scriptural texts in which biblical figures are similarly marginalized; to evaluate how Scripture is being interpreted and whether the church is responding with love and compassion to marginalized people; and then to act in solidarity with those who are marginalized.

The consultation allowed for interaction in a number of formats from one-on-one discussion, group work, and regional groups, to open plenary sessions which consequently created space for fairly in-depth conversation—a process of truly meeting the "other." Something that stood out from this consultation, as a result of painful personal narratives, but also from the consultation's insistence on privacy and confidentiality, was the price that some had to pay for "coming out"; but perhaps more alarming, the price some had to pay for merely "speaking out." The power of the church as an important institution, especially in Africa, upholding heteronormative discourse became clear in the genuine fear and anxiety of some participants, as the threat of suspension and even excommunication as a result

17. The Consultation gathered from July 29–August 1, 2013.

of risking counter-dominant opinion or actions of solidarity, was clear and present. Being a religious leader within a community is for most not only a calling but also the way to secure a sustainable livelihood. It should therefore come as no surprise that although some feel deep compassion with their homosexual brothers and sisters within African communities, they simply cannot risk "speaking out," and as a result find themselves out in the cold. The consultation brought together those who had the courage and conviction to speak out and bear the consequences, but also those who have sympathy but who choose to conduct their resistance in a more strategic way, thus speaking when it is possible and trying to change dominant opinion from the inside. Both approaches have very real consequences as those who "speak out" openly can find themselves without a job (and the resulting security) and those who conduct resistance more overtly live in constant fear of being found out by the dominant powers, or of being branded unfaithful by those living the counter-normative.

Negotiation of the Legitimization Process in the Dutch Reformed Church

A second example that comes from my South African context is the negotiation of the legitimization process[18] for lesbian and gay students within the Dutch Reformed Church (DRC) at Stellenbosch University. The result of the church-sanctioned legitimization process concerns a change in status when theological students become eligible to be called into positions of public ministry. The process of legitimization at Stellenbosch University for DRC students brings together as conversation partners the prospective candidate, the Theological Faculty Council to reflect and report on the prospective candidate's academic competence, and the Curatorium (a decision-making body charged with overseeing theological education and ministry formation) of the DRC. Conversations and discussions around the legitimization of gay and lesbian students are bound by the 2007 decision[19] on homosexuality by the General Synod of the DRC.

18. A church-sanctioned process that declares candidates ready for ordination into church ministry.

19. The 2007 General Synod decision on homosexuality, which represented a remarkable progression in the Dutch Reformed Church position on the issue of homosexuality, stated the following: Firstly that the Bible is the church's main source document and that any contemplation on the issue of homosexuality should start from a biblical basis. Interpreters should honestly reflect on contemporary issues, such as homosexuality, in

According to the position that was adopted by the DRC in 2007, it follows that openly gay theology students can be legitimized and can enter into positions within ministry as long as they commit to a life of celibacy. In order to practically enforce this policy, prospective gay/lesbian candidates to ministry have to make some sort of public statement that would commit them to a life of celibacy.

In practice, this theoretical guideline hypothetically gives rise to the following possible scenarios:[20] First, gay students who have the gift of celibacy can publicly commit to a life spent in ministry, regardless of the double standard inherent in the policy that expects only gay students to engage in such a decision. Second, a gay student can openly declare their sexual orientation and their relational status and thereby forfeit the opportunity to be legitimized within the church. Openly declaring one's gay orientation and relational status and continuing the process towards legitimization brings one in direct conflict with the church's policy and has the potential to become a full-fledged confrontation with the full consequence of media attention and public opinion.[21] Finally, a gay student can decide

the light of biblical values. Secondly, the love of Christ is the basis for all relationships within the faith community. All human beings are created to the image of God; all are included in the salvation obtained by Christ and party to the gift of the Holy Spirit. The human dignity of all is reaffirmed. Thirdly, all people, regardless of sexual orientation, are included in the love of God and become part of the church through baptism and faith. Being part of the church implies access to the sacraments, admittance into different church offices, and the subjection to church discipline. Fourthly, marriage as institution is reserved for heterosexual people as it is seen (in line with the 2004 General Synod Decision) as the union between one man and one woman. Fifthly, both homo- and heterosexual promiscuity are strongly rejected. As a sixth point it is stated that the status of civil union partnerships of gay people are not equitable to the institution of marriage. Under point 7 the authority of the General Synod to make decisions about a candidate's eligibility to become clergy is reaffirmed. The General Synod states that legitimized homosexual candidates can become clergy as long as they live a life of celibacy. Finally the decision states that different individual church councils can engage in issues pertaining to homosexuality in their own unique way, as long as it is done in the spirit of Christian love. The statement showed remarkable wisdom at the time in somehow bringing together the voices of two opposing camps, but also that has proved to be insufficient, as a number of real-life situations have shown the inconsistencies within the decision and the life-denying realities that it had as a consequence.

20. This is naturally not an all-inclusive list, as life is sometimes stranger than fiction and realities develop that cannot be dreamed up from the comfort of an academic vantage point. I am also very aware of the fact that the scenarios sketched in this paper are academic and hypothetical, but for those who live these and other painful realities, each scenario has a price tag, and the price can sometimes be inconceivable.

21. A case in point: On November 30, 2011 the Afrikaans daily newspaper *Die Burger*

not to "come out" publicly and to make no overt commitments to any form of gay/lesbian gender identity. One could go all out in not "coming out" by saying nothing to anyone or one can choose to selectively share identity information in safe spaces. By stating nothing and entering into a "don't ask, don't tell" relationship with the Curatorium, one can be legitimized and consequently be called into public ministry. Living closeted in public ministry implies increased risk of being "out-ed" by others and almost inevitably leads to risk behavior. But, the situatedness of an alternative voice and opinion within the confines of the heteronormative structure holds unprecedented potential for transformation when the hidden or masked "other" potentially becomes the beloved.

Although all of the above-mentioned decisions carry a price tag, the third option especially seems rife with complications as it holds possible resistance, on a personal level, in relation to fellow marginalized and those who were unaware of an *outsider* being *in*. Not making any identity statements can lead to feelings of falseness and a possible disconnection between private and public personae. Beyond the internal tension this position can lead to great anxiety as a result of the fear of being found out and called out in public, not to mention the traumatic relational consequences if one is "out-ed" by a friend or acquaintance. In terms of fellow marginalized who choose to take a more public position, the potential risk exists for being blamed for not taking a stand against situations or institutions of oppression.

From the above-mentioned exposition, it is clear that the negotiation of queer identity within a heteronormative society/church is complex and often dangerous, as safe spaces are difficult to find. "Speaking out" and

---

ran a front page story on Lulani Vermeulen, a 29 year old, white, Afrikaans-speaking, lesbian theological student who was, according to the article, denied legitimization by the Curatorium of the Dutch Reformed Church, after successfully completing her theological studies at Stellenbosch University. In the days that followed the initial article, the complexities and intricacies of the decision and the situation that led to the decision by the Curatorium became more apparent. Although Lulani completed her BTh degree in 2009, her MDiv in 2010 and her Licentiate in Theology in 2011, thereby obtaining the academic qualifications necessary for admittance into ministry, she was refused legitimization (a church-sanctioned process that declares candidates ready for ordination into church ministry) because she would not sign a document stating that she would live a life of celibacy. A prerequisite only expected of her (and not of her heterosexual classmates) because of her sexual orientation. Her refusal to sign the document on the basis of her conviction of the injustice of the request and the lived reality of her committed same-sex partner relationship left the Curatorium, according to their assessment, with "no other choice" than to deny her the possibility of legitimization.

"coming out" is a risky business: Revealing too much too soon can leave one sidelined, voiceless, or nullified. Revealing too little too late easily leads to one being accused of public and private falseness, lying, and betrayal. In the process of "coming out," questions abound: What to say? If anything, to whom to say it and how to say it?

It is with all of these issues of complexity and especially with consideration of the accusation of deceit often voiced when one was thought to be *in*, and then suddenly comes *out*, that I approach a close reading of Tamar's story in Genesis 38. This narrative is particularly intriguing for the discussion on "coming out," as Tamar is also portrayed as one who skillfully, in the process of hiding and revealing, negotiates her identity and ultimately succeeds in unmasking an unjust system.

COMING OUT IN GENESIS 38

I would like to structure my engagement with the Tamar story in Genesis 38 around three central themes in the narrative which seem particularly important for further ethical reflection. These moments in the Tamar story may serve as conversation starters when the text is used as a reflective surface for modern readers engaged in the tricky process of identity negotiation.

Firstly, Tamar's trickery is explained against the backdrop of her vulnerable, voiceless, and powerless situation due to the lack of protection in the patriarchal social construction. In Gen 38:1–11, the narrative stage is set by describing the process leading to Tamar's position of vulnerability.

The story begins with breathtaking pace as Judah moves away from his brothers and settles in Canaanite territory. The progression in time is communicated via Judah's experience of major life events as we are told that he marries a local girl and that three sons (Er, Onan, and Shelah) are born from their union. Up until the end of verse 5, everything happens as expected and Judah's move to Canaan seems prosperous as his wife, in proper response, conceives, gives birth, and names the sons. Judah is the main character in the first eleven verses as he functions, as Van Wijk-Bos states, as "the sun around which the satellites of family and friends move. He sees, he takes, he impregnates."[22]

In verse 6, Tamar is introduced as the wife chosen for the eldest son, Er. We do not know much about Er, except that he "erred" in the eyes of the Lord

22. Van Wijk-Bos, "Out of the Shadows," 44.

and that YHWH puts him to death. The expectation of the reader is interrupted as one would expect the narrative to continue along the same fertile and fruitful lines as it did with Judah. The death of Er and the childlessness of Tamar produce the enticing moment in the narrative as she is left vulnerable and without protection. Judah, who is now responsible for Tamar according to custom, instructs Onan to undertake a levirate marriage with Tamar, the customary practice of marrying the widow of one's childless brother to maintain his line and to ensure the widow's future, as required by ancient Hebrew law to protect the most vulnerable. Amit elaborates on the protection implied by the cultural practice when stating: "In biblical times, this law implied a major economic advantage for the childless widow who might have been left out in the cold but, through levirate marriage, was able to continue participating in the family circle of her dead husband."[23] In contrast, Onan acts against the protective intention of the cultural practice when he abuses Tamar in her position of vulnerability.[24] Besides Tamar, God bears witness to this deception and Onan is put to death.

At this point, it is important to note that the reader is privy to information that is unknown to Judah. Kruschwitz notes that "the reader knows YHWH's part in the death of Er and Onan. In contrast to the reader, Judah believes the union with Tamar to result in death.[25] As a result he perpetrates his act of deception, sending her home to her father as a widow while misleading her to believe that Shelah will perform his levirate duty when he grows up."[26] The first act of deception in this story is thus perpetrated by Judah as he fails to act as Tamar's custodian and neglects the protecting custom of levirate marriage that was supposed to bring Tamar security in a husband and offspring. Both Onan and Judah act in such a way as

---

23. Amit, "The Case of Judah and Tamar," 218.

24. Terrence Fretheim elaborates when stating: "Onan sabotages the intent of the relationship in order to gain Er's inheritance for himself upon Judah's death—the firstborn would receive a double share. He regularly uses Tamar for sex, but makes sure she does not become pregnant by not letting his semen into her (*coitus interruptus*) . . . He thereby formally fulfills his duty, lest the role be passed on to his other brother and he loses Er's inheritance in this way," "Genesis," 605.

25. Fretheim elaborates by stating: "Judah, having lost two sons and perhaps wondering whether Tamar were the problem, seeks to protect his own future by keeping his last son from her. He does so at Tamar's expense, directing her to return to her own father's house, where she would not have inheritance rights or be free to remarry. This act cuts her off from her husband's family and places her future welfare in jeopardy," "Genesis," 605.

26. Kruschwitz, "The Type-Scene Connection," 398.

to refuse Tamar that to which she is entitled, and Tamar finds herself the vulnerable victim of others' deceptive acts. Arnold further explores Tamar's vulnerability when stating: "Tamar has been wronged and is desperate. She has been abandoned and perhaps branded a dangerous woman—an unmarriageable, childless widow—perhaps the most vulnerable state of ancient Semitic society."[27] From the above, it is clear that the safety net of the patriarchal system fails Tamar and that the reality that the widowed Tamar has to conform to when sent home by Judah is life-denying. Tamar's act of trickery should be understood against this backdrop. Tamar is voiceless, as illustrated in the text, and power or might is not at her disposal, so she employs wit and cunning in devising a plot of deception to achieve her desired end. Tamar as a trickster has a low social status, prohibiting gain or advancement through means available to others. To a certain extent Tamar is left with no other choice but to explore, albeit it devious, alternative options. The story thus illustrates that where no other means are possible (where people are rendered voiceless and powerless, nullified by the social structure), trickery is inevitable.

Tamar's vulnerability within the patriarchal system seems a comparable reality to that experienced by queer people in a dominant heteronormative society. Virginia Mollenkott describes the position of queer people in the church as "low and outside." She goes on to argue, "Those who find themselves disadvantaged, on the 'outside', in the margins as it were, make use of trickery and other forms of manipulative behavior (like gossip, misinformation, nagging, playing possum, distractions, and deceptions) because they do not have what sociologists refer to as 'assigned power.'"[28] Within the occupied territory of church and ministry, when the power brokers simply will not listen and when the center forgets the margin, it seems inevitable that the disenfranchised will resort to some form of trickery.

Secondly, Tamar's trickery implies deception as she hides her true identity in order to perform another role. Tamar transforms herself from being a passive object to one who unmasks injustice through her performance. Robert Alter remarks that until this point in the narrative, "Tamar has been a passive object, acted upon—or alas, not acted upon—by Judah and his sons. The only verbs she was the subject of were the two verbs of compliance and retreat, to go off and dwell, at the end of verse 11."[29]

27. Arnold, *Genesis*, 327.

28. Mollenkott, "Reading the Bible," 13.

29. Alter, *The Art of Biblical Narrative*, 8.

In a dramatic act of *peripeteia*,[30] the deceived becomes the deceiver as Tamar realizes the reality of her situation and resorts to deceptive behavior of her own. Tamar's act of deception that starts with the removal of her garments of widowhood, earns her the designation of trickster. As Susan Niditch[31] says it well:

> One of the biblical authors' favorite narrative patterns is that of the trickster. Israelites tend to portray their ancestors and thereby to imagine themselves as underdogs, as people outside the establishment who achieve success in roundabout, irregular ways. One of the ways the marginal confronts those in power and achieve their goals is through deception or trickery. The improvement of their status may be only temporary, for to be a trickster is to be of unstable status, to be involved in transformation and change.[32]

Tamar's act of trickery implies a temporary discontinuation from her status as "widow" when she takes off her widow's garments[33] and begins a veiled performance as a prostitute. Garments in this story have the power to conceal or reveal identity. The veil that functions as an instrumental prop in her performance conceals her true identity.[34] By taking up the harlot's

---

30. According to narrative theory, the moment of *peripetea* in a narrative is a unique turning point when a reversal of circumstances takes place.

31. Niditch outlines the five-step trickster morphology: (1) problem: the hero has low status; (2) plan: a deception is schemed to improve status/conditions; (3) execution: the plan is executed and results in improved status/condition; (4) complications: the deception is uncovered; and (5) outcome; the hero subsequently experiences a reduction of status, but survive, *A Prelude to Biblical Folklore*, 42–45.

32. Niditch, "Genesis," 36.

33. There is an important link to the Joseph story with regard to a strong shared garment motif. Fentress-Williams states: "As is the case in the surrounding Joseph narrative garments conveys status, position and favor, or role. They also have the power to conceal or reveal identity. In the story of Joseph, the robe his father gives him is a visible sign of favor, and that same robe is used to deceive Jacob about his beloved son's death. . . . Similarly, Tamar's new garments apparently conceal her identity from Judah, who mistakes her for a prostitute," "Location," 63.

34. While not saying that Tamar dressed as a prostitute, the text implies that the dress and posture she adopted made her easily taken for one. Van Wolde continues along the same line: "Tamar takes off her widow's clothes, veils herself and sits down in the city gate. There is no ambivalence at all; it is clear that she acts as a whore, because women are not supposed to sit in the gate. When Judah passes, he immediately assumes she is a whore. And Tamar acts accordingly, starting to bargain with Judah, as is usually done in these cases," "Intertextuality," 447. Cf. also Fentress-Williams, "Location," 64.

veil, Tamar actively and consciously portrays a role other than that of marginalized and powerless widow.

Tamar's risky/active/deceiving performance is so convincing that it is repeatedly stated that Judah did not recognize her as his daughter-in-law. He did not know her. Judah mistakes Tamar for a prostitute. For a second time, Judah is the one who sees but who lacks understanding. Just as his reasoning failed him with the death of his sons, so again he fails to recognize the truth right in front of his eyes at Enaim-gate or "the gate of the eyes" where Tamar starts the process of revealing the truth.[35]

Tamar uses perceptions and misperceptions about her identity to achieve her goal. The performance that Tamar renders from behind the veil affords her a voice in the negotiation process, as she bargains for a gift. She does not proceed with the matters at hand, but demands a pledge. Judah hands over the intimate markers of his identity and has sexual intercourse with Tamar. Tamar, having conceived, returns home and continues her previous identity by dressing in her widows garments (vv. 15–19).

Reflecting on Tamar's trickery, it is important to note that Tamar as the powerless widow does not cease to exist but is hidden under the mask she adopts as a prop in the veiled part that she consciously chooses to portray. She takes up this part in an active attempt to unmask the injustice that is done to her by the hands of a system that has failed her, but more specifically at the hands of Judah and his sons.

It is especially this aspect of the story that may help queer people within the church to reflect on the position that they take up within structures that usually would not allow them to have a voice or would automatically negate the value of their experience. Tamar hides or masks the truth of her own vulnerability in order to unmask a situation of injustice. Perhaps the same tricky reasoning can be applied to vulnerable outsiders who consciously choose to tell a queer lie to reveal a straight truth. Perhaps this part of the story holds the strongest potential to be an emancipatory reflective surface to those who choose to play a masked or veiled part within powerful excluding structures.

---

35. Van Wijk-Bos states: "The new stationing (at the roadside) marks the turning point of Tamar's role in the story and indicates an active waiting instead of an obedient response to the male who rules over her. Tamar sits at the 'eye opener' by her own choice; she is not sent here as she had been sent home by Judah. So she sits and waits, wrapped in clothes that give a clear sexual signal; she, who had been dependent on the approaches of the men around her in regards to her sexual life, takes matters into her own hands," "Out of the Shadows," 45.

Thirdly, it is in the moment of recognition that transformation takes place and right relationships are restored. The moment to which the entire narrative builds up is the moment in which Judah truly sees himself and as a result can truly see Tamar. All the misconceptions and false images that Judah created of Tamar are shattered as he sees himself, as he sees her. Judah sees in Tamar one misunderstood, falsely accused, rendered voiceless, unprotected, but perhaps Judah sees beyond that one who longs for life, for relationship, for future.

The moment of recognition is set up in vv. 20–23 when Judah is told that Tamar acted as a prostitute and is pregnant. Kruschwitz remarks: "At this point, before Judah comes to acknowledge his wrongdoing, he remains unconcerned with Tamar's plight. Judah remains enmeshed in his ignorance. Still not recognizing that his own daughter-in-law played the harlot with him, he behaves in a manner completely inappropriate to the reality of the situation."[36]

Tamar, certainly now at her most vulnerable, replies to Judah's judgment by asking him to "please recognize" to whom these belong, namely the seal and the cord and the staff (v. 25). Kruschwitz rightly comments on the pivotal moment of recognition that "Tamar's message does not invite Judah to recognize first who she is, but rather who he is. By coming to terms with his own identity and past behavior, Judah of course cannot avoid then recognizing her whom he has wronged."[37] Judah finally takes a close look and sees. "Faced with himself he is able to see both himself and Tamar. He sees that what he should have given he did not give and that which he gave set the trap to show his own unrighteousness."[38] Judah sees and recognizes that Tamar is "more right than I am." The moment of *anagnorisis* (the moment when one character comes to recognize the true identity of another character) brings about a restoration in the relationship.[39]

It is precisely this instant of recognition that Juliana Claassens alludes to in her essay "Resisting Dehumanization: Ruth, Tamar, and the quest for Human Dignity." She states that the act of "Seeing the Face of the Other,"

---

36. Kruschwitz, "The Type-Scene Connection," 405.

37. Ibid., 406.

38. Van Wijk-Bos, "Out of the Shadows," 47.

39. Kruschwitz alludes to this moment in the Tamar/Judah story: "Effecting a dramatic change in character relations, *anagnorisis* leads the parties who have stood against one another throughout the story to reconcile. Enemies become friends, outcasts become family." In the Tamar story, "*anagnorisis* helps bind together familial ties that have come undone," "The Type-Scene Connection," 407.

as one of the sections in her essay is titled, functions as the moment for the restoration of human dignity. She states:

> In both stories, it is in the face-to-face encounter that the possibility of transformation occurs. This transformation takes place only when the male characters (the powerful), in response to the women's actions of resistance to the violation of their dignity, recognize the common humanity of the women in front of them. It is by means of transcendence through empathy that the male protagonist comprehends that there is a human—a woman—behind the veil, that the status quo can be confronted, and that new possibilities for engagement emerge.[40]

Judah is called in the moment of revelation not to recognize Tamar, but rather to recognize *himself* and the injustice he had done to her. The moment calls for self-recognition on the part of the powerful when Judah has to admit that through his actions and in his process of decision making he has denied Tamar life, love, and the possibility to flourish. The deceiving act of the powerless victim thus unmasks the injustice committed by the perpetrator. Judah can only see Tamar when he has seen himself. In the same way, dominant heteronormative institutions and representatives of those institutions will only be able to see queer others the moment that they see themselves. New and life-giving ways to deal with diversity will only develop when the powerful see the injustice their silencing and sidelining in dominant discourse creates.

CONCLUSION

Tamar's story of powerlessness, deceit, and recognition seems a relevant and powerful reflective surface for queer voices within a reality constructed on heteronormative assumptions. Hiding, trickery, and deception employed by queer people is often met with harsh judgments of untruthfulness; verdicts rendered from the mainline as well as from the margin. A remarkable aspect of the Tamar story is the apparent lack of judgment on the means employed by Tamar to unmask the injustice that she suffers. Although the means employed by Tamar would in normal circumstances not be judged in a positive light, neither the text nor the narrator and not even the victim of her deception (Judah) seems in any way to condemn Tamar for her actions. In fact, Judah declares Tamar more righteous than himself.

40. Claassens, "Resisting Dehumanization," 671.

Obviously the aim of this essay is not to encourage dishonesty and deceit, but rather to engage with the realities of exclusion, shaming, and silencing that often leaves vulnerable individuals with no other choice but to render a performance that will reveal the truth. Ultimately beyond the very real need for tricking and deceiving in the midst of complex social realities, the very real need for recognition exists. For, it is in the moment of recognition that the possibility for restored human dignity exists.

The title of this essay comes from the fourth single release for Snow Patrol's sixth album, *Fallen Empires*. Lead singer Gary Lightbody explains the track's meaning to *Billboard Magazine*: "This song is about kind of realizing what the truth is. Realizing, kind of, that all that matters is having love in your life, be it family, friends, a girlfriend or a boyfriend and that everything can be boiled down to that and maybe that is the meaning of life."

In moments of recognition we might discover our common humanity, and the common longings of our heart—the longing for life, love, and togetherness, future . . . because perhaps Lightbody is on to something when he says: "In the end, in the end, there is nothing more to life than love, is there?"

BIBLIOGRAPHY

Ackermann, Denise. *Tamar's Cry: Re-reading an Ancient Text in the Midst of an HIV/AIDS Pandemic*. Stellenbosch: Ecumenical Foundation of Southern Africa, 2001.

Alter, Robert. *The Art of Biblical Narrative*. New York: Basic, 1981.

Amit, Yairah. "The Case of Judah and Tamar in the Contemporary Israeli Context: A Relevant Interpolation." In *Genesis: Texts@Contexts*, edited by Athalya Brenner, Archie Chi Chung Lee, and Gale A. Yee, 213–20. Minneapolis: Fortress, 2010.

Arnold, Bill T. *Genesis*. The New Cambridge Bible Commentary. Cambridge: Cambridge University Press, 2009.

Cheng, Patrick S. *Radical Love: An Introduction to Queer Theology*. New York: Church Publishing, 2011.

Claassens, L. Juliana. "Resisting Dehumanization: Ruth, Tamar, and the Quest for Human Dignity." *Catholic Biblical Quarterly* 74 (2012) 659–74.

Di Silvio, Lorenzo. "Correcting Corrective Rape: Carmichele and Developing South Africa's Affirmative Obligations to Prevent Violence Against Women." *Georgetown Law Journal* 99 (2010) 1469–1515.

Fentress-Williams, Judy. "Location, Location, Location: Tamar in the Joseph Cycle." In *Bakhtin and Genre Theory in Biblical Studies*, edited by Roland Boer, Semeia 63, 63–68. Atlanta: Society of Biblical Literature, 2007.

Fretheim, Terence E. "The Book of Genesis." In *The New Interpreter's Bible: A Commentary in Twelve Volumes*, edited by Leander E. Keck, Vol. 1, 319–673. Nashville, TN: Abingdon, 1994.

Hauerwas, Stanley. "Christians in the Hands of Flaccid Secularists. Theology and 'Moral Inquiry' in the Modern University." *Ethical Perspectives* 4/2 (1997) 32–47.

Jordan, Karen M., and Robert H. Deluty. "Coming Out for Lesbian Women: Its Relation to Anxiety, Positive Affectivity, Self-esteem, and Social Support." *Journal of Homosexuality* 35/2 (1998) 41–63.

Kessler, Rainer. "From Bipolar to Multipolar Understanding." In *Through the Eyes of Another: Intercultural Reading of the Bible*, edited by J. Hans De Wit, Louis C. Jonker, Marleen Kool, and Daniel Schipani, 452–59. Elkhart, IN: Institute of Mennonite Studies, 2004.

Kruschwitz, Jonathan. "The Type-Scene Connection between Genesis 38 and the Joseph Story." *JSOT* 36/4 (2012) 383–410.

Lapsley, Jacqueline. E. *Whispering the Word: Hearing Women's Stories in the Old Testament.* Louisville: Westminster John Knox, 2005.

Martin, Andrew, Annie Kelley, Laura Turquet, and Stephanie Ross. *Hate Crimes: The Rise of "Corrective" Rape in South Africa*, 1–18. Online: https://www.actionaid.org.uk/ sites/default/files/doc_lib/correctiveraperep_final.pdf

Mollenkott, Virginia. R. "Reading the Bible from Low and Outside. Lesbitransgay People as God's Tricksters." In *Take Back the Word: A Queer Reading of the Bible*, edited by Robert E. Goss and Mona West, 13–22. Cleveland, OH: Pilgrim, 2000.

Niditch, Susan. "Genesis." In *The Women's Bible Commentary*, edited by Carol A. Newsom, Sharon H. Ringe, and Jacqueline E. Lapsley, 27–45. 3rd ed. Louisville, KY: Westminster John Knox, 2012.

————. *A Prelude to Biblical Folklore: Underdogs and Tricksters.* Urbana, IL: University of Chicago Press, 2000.

Petersen, Robin. "Theological and Religious Pluralism." In *Doing Theology in Context: South African Perspectives*, edited by John De Gruchy and Charles Villa-Vicencio, 219–28. Maryknoll: Orbis, 1994.

Schneider, Laurel C. "Queer Theory." In *Handbook of Postmodern Biblical Interpretation*, edited by Andrew K. M. Adam, 206–12. St Louis, MO: Chalice, 2000.

Seow, Choon-Leong. "Textual Orientation." In *Biblical Ethics and Homosexuality: Listening to Scripture*, edited by Robert L. Brawley, 17–34. Louisville, KY: Westminster/John Knox, 1996.

Togarasei, Lovemore, and Ezra Chitando. "Beyond the Bible: Critical Reflections on the Contributions of Cultural and Postcolonial Studies on Same-sex Relationships in Africa." *Journal of Gender and Religion in Africa* 17/2 (2011) 109–25.

Tutu, Desmond. "Foreword." In *Aliens in the Household of God: Homosexuality and Christian Faith in South Africa*, edited by Paul Germond and Steve De Gruchy, no pages. Cape Town: David Philip, 1997.

Van Wijk-Bos, Johanna W. H. "Out of the Shadows: Genesis 38; Judges 4:17–22; Ruth 3." In *Reasoning with the Foxes: Female Wit in a World of Male Power*, edited by J. Cheryl Exum and Johanna W. H. van Wijk-Bos. Semeia 42, 37–67. Atlanta: Society of Biblical Literature, 1988.

Van Wolde, Ellen. "Intertextuality: Ruth in Dialogue with Tamar." In *A Feminist Companion to Reading the Bible: Approaches, Methods and Strategies*, edited by Athalya Brenner and Carole Fontaine, 426–51. Sheffield, UK: Sheffield Academic Press, 1997.

Yep, Gust, Karen E. Lovaas, and John P. Elia. *Queer Theory and Communication: From Disciplining Queers to Queering the Discipline(s).* New York: Harrington Park, 2003.

5

Contending for Dignity in the Bible and the Post-Apartheid South African Public Realm

Gerald West,
School of Religion, Philosophy,
and Classics & Ujamaa Centre,
University of KwaZulu-Natal

INTRODUCTION

In the recent South African film, *Son of Man*, a retelling of the Gospel story of Jesus set in postliberation South Africa, Jesus addresses the crowd in a shack settlement. Standing on top of a VIP (Ventilated Improved Pit latrine) toilet, Jesus delivers this film's version of Matthew's "sermon on the mount" (or part of it) (0:47.35).[1] While armed soldiers loiter in the background and a military helicopter hovers overhead, Jesus says (in isiXhosa), "My people, we have deliberately chosen to operate openly. Let us work together,

---

1. *Son of Man* (2006). Directed by Mark Dornford-May. Produced by Dimpho di Kopane.

because through collective dialogue we can penetrate the deafest of ears." As the crowd roars its approval, he continues, saying, "It feels like we are defeated. We need to act like a movement to ensure that each of us is treated with dignity." Again, the crowd roars its approval. Jesus continues, saying, "Let us unite. Solidarity! Unity!" The crowd embraces this call, breaking into collaborative song and dance, led by rhythmic drumming on a rubbish bin. This collective action draws more soldiers, and the order is given to disperse. Some of the crowd begins to move away, but one of the disciples (Peter) picks up a lump of concrete and advances on the soldiers. Jesus instructs him to drop the concrete, but makes it clear to the soldiers by his stance and stare that they are not backing down. Glaring down at them from the top of the toilet Jesus stands with feet apart and arms flexed at his side. He then climbs down from the toilet, slowly. Once on the ground he pauses, confronting the soldiers with his dignity, before turning his back on them and joining the crowd. The hidden transcript of dignity has taken public form.

This is the turning point of this film's portrayal of Jesus, for following this confrontation Judas takes the video-taped evidence of the organizing and mobilizing activities of Jesus to the neocolonial leaders who are plotting his death. And while there is much in this film that worries me,[2] the moment when Jesus reminds the people of their dignity rings true both to our context and the Gospels. Jesus, both in this film and in portions of the Gospel accounts, recognizes that dignity resides both in the individual and in their collaborative action in the public realm.

In an attempt to understand the sociology of the early Jesus movement, Richard Horsley has argued that the Q material common to Matthew and Luke, of which the so-called sermon on the mount (Matthew)/plain (Luke) forms a part, comes from a community that sees itself in continuity with the hopes of "Israel."[3] For the Q community, a particular trajectory of "Israel" is being recovered and restored through Jesus, who is the organic intellectual of the "Jesus movement." According to Horsley, the "Israel" that is being renewed under the coming or presence of "the kingdom of God" is not, on the one hand, concerned about maintaining boundaries over against the Gentiles; it is not an ethnic project. On the other hand, the "Israel" of the Q people "is defined over against Jerusalem and representatives of the government and official traditions, and participation is based

2. West, "The *Son of Man* in South Africa?"

3. Horsley, *Sociology and the Jesus Movement*, 110–11.

not on one's proper lineage as children of Abraham but on repentance and action according to the teachings of Jesus (Q/Luke 3:7–9; 6:46–49, etc.)." In particular, argues Horsley, "the Q people understand John [the Baptist] and Jesus as the climactic figures in the line of the prophets who, almost by definition, stood over against and were rejected by the ruling institutions and their representatives (Q/Luke 7:18–35; 11:47–51; 13:34–35)."[4]

Something similar is clearly taking place in the *Son of Man* film, and dignity is identified as a key resource. I am interested in how dignity is configured in this twofold struggle: the formation of community on the one side and the related resistance to domination on the other side.

THE OLD TESTAMENT'S PROPHETIC TRAJECTORY

Within biblical scholarship there have been regular attempts to analyze the contending voices within biblical texts. Norman Gottwald's work on early "Israel" was among the pioneering work in this area, and although the focus of this work had a strong historical and sociological emphasis,[5] his later work did use this socio-historical analysis to discern contending voices in the literary productions themselves.[6] Robert Coote's work on Amos was perhaps the most sustained project of this kind, including socio-historical, literary, and even theological analysis.[7] Both Gottwald's and Coote's work was taken up by South African biblical scholar Itumeleng Mosala,[8] and his contribution produced a seismic shift in South African and North American black theology, inaugurating what Tinyiko Maluleke refers to as a second wave of South African black theology,[9] in which the Bible is no longer a monovocal resource on the side of the liberation struggle. Within this scholarly tradition, the early (1990s) work of Walter Brueggemann has been particularly suggestive in sketching both the socio-historical and literary-ideological dimensions of the Bible's contending voices.[10] Coote's

---

4. Horsley, *Sociology and the Jesus Movement*, 111.

5. Gottwald, *The Tribes of Yahweh*.

6. Gottwald, *The Hebrew Bible*.

7. Coote, *Amos among the Prophets*.

8. Mosala, *Biblical Hermeneutics and Black Theology in South Africa*.

9. Maluleke, "Black Theology as Public Discourse."

10. Brueggemann, "A Shape for Old Testament Theology, I"; Brueggemann, "A Shape for Old Testament Theology, II"; Brueggemann, "Trajectories in Old Testament Literature and the Sociology of Ancient Israel."

four-layered analysis of "biblical voices" is probably closer to the realities of ancient (and modern) struggles, but Brueggemann's two trajectories offer a heuristic entry point into both the socio-historical and literary dimensions of not only the Old Testament/Hebrew Bible, but also the New Testament. Indeed, the recognition that such trajectories continue through the testaments has been a significant contribution in itself, one that has been taken up by Horsley in his notion of "renewal."

What Horsley reconstructs as the ideology of the Q community is in continuity with Brueggemann's "prophetic trajectory," i.e., "a movement of protest which is situated among the disinherited and which articulates its theological vision in terms of a God who decisively intrudes, even against seemingly impenetrable institutions and orderings," and stands over against what Brueggemann refers to as the "consolidatory trajectory," i.e., "a movement of consolidation which is situated among the established and secure and which articulates its theological vision in terms of a God who faithfully abides and sustains on behalf of the present ordering."[11]

As Horsley argues, the communities of the Jesus movement thought of themselves as "a new social order,"[12] but a social order that both breaks with consolidatory formations and stands in continuity with prophetic forces. Indeed, Horsley's particular contribution lies in his recognition and analysis of the contending nature of this "renewal" project. In a world full of various tensions, the "fundamental conflict in Jewish Palestine was not between the different layers of political-economic (religious) rulers, but between the ruling groups [both domestic and foreign] on the one hand and the bulk of the people on the other."[13]

Horsley argues that the primary ethic of the Jesus movement and their renewal project was an internal ethic. In Acts, Paul, and Q, Horsley detects such an ethic. For example, instead of the consolidatory control of patriarchal authority, the emerging Jesus community developed its own procedures for resolving disputes and conflicts among themselves (see Luke 6:37–42 and 17:1–2, 3–4, as well as Luke 12:58–59/Matt 5:25–26 and Matt 18:15–20). As Horsley goes on to note, the ethic of Matt 18:15–20 is strikingly similar to that of "the rigorously disciplined community as Qumran (1QS 5:25—6:1; CD 9:2–8)," which suggests, he argues, "that we have here

---

11. Brueggemann, "Trajectories in Old Testament Literature and the Sociology of Ancient Israel," 202.

12. Horsley, *Sociology and the Jesus Movement*, 122.

13. Ibid., 85.

not some 'higher ideal' but rather procedures actually practiced by local communities of the Jesus movement."[14]

Indeed, as Horsley points out, "One of the features of the churches that most impressed later pagan observers, even opponents such as Celsus or Lucian, was the Christians' concrete care of each other."[15] The sayings tradition of Q includes ample evidence "that Jesus and/or his movement were concerned for the concrete alleviation of hunger, debt, and other symptoms of poverty."[16] The "sermon" material in Luke 12:22–31/Matthew 6:25–33 is a good example of this, calling for an internal ethic of the renewal of reciprocity. This is not primary an external ethic, directed to those outside the community, but first and foremost an internal "local" socio-economic ethic.[17] The internal ethic is structured around the affirmation of dignity and solidarity among the marginalized; the external ethic is derived from and resourced by this internal ethic.

It is the primacy and priority of an internal community ethic that the *Son of Man* film emphasizes. What the *Son of Man* film makes overt is the implicit place of dignity in this ethic. In the next section of this essay, I analyze in some depth the central place that dignity has come to hold in our postliberation social movements.

ABAHLALI BASEMJONDOLO

The place of dignity in our contemporary struggle, nearly twenty years after political liberation, is clearly expressed in the Abahlali baseMjondolo movement. On March 19, 2005, a group of black shack dwellers barricaded a major road in Durban, KwaZulu-Natal, South Africa. Like so many other "service delivery" protests, a sign of our times, this action was a protest against the failure of the state to deliver housing for the Kennedy Road shack dwellers. They had been promised that houses would be built for them on a nearby piece of land, enabling them to move from their shack settlement crammed between the Clare Estate and the Bisasar rubbish dump.[18] But under pressure from developers the promise of homes was broken, and the community was threatened with forced removal "to a place

14. Ibid., 123–24.

15. Ibid., 124.

16. Ibid.

17. Ibid., 124–25.

18. Gibson, *Fanonian Practices in South Africa*, 144.

miles outside the city, far from work opportunities, schools, hospitals, and the communities they had been a part of."[19] As bulldozers moved in to level "their 'Promised Land'" (the biblical image is theirs),[20] the community acted, barricading Umgeni Road with their bodies, and burning tires. More than seven hundred shack dwellers participated in this protest action, and despite a vigorous police response, two days later, on March 21, 2005, Human Rights Day (and the anniversary of the 1960 Sharpeville massacre), more than a thousand demonstrated, demanding that the police release those who had been arrested.

In his in-depth study of Abahlali baseMjondolo, Nigel Gibson argues that by March 2005 the shack dwellers had become a social movement, "by virtue of their self-organization and by developing their own relationships with other shack dwellers." As he argues:

> The development of such horizontal links among the shack settlements suggested a new kind of movement in the making. By May 2005, the people from Kennedy Road and five other shack settlements, as well as residents from local municipal flats, organized a march of over 3 000 people. With banners expressing their collective will ("We want our land") and homegrown political education ("The University of Kennedy Road"), the marchers presented a memorandum of ten demands that they had drawn up through a series of meetings and community discussions (see Patel 2008).[21] Written by the shack and flat dwellers after careful discussion, this memorandum, which included the need for housing, jobs, sanitation, medical care, education and safety from police brutality and environmental toxins, became a people's charter—one that sought to represent not only Durban's 800 000 shack dwellers, but the poor across South Africa, where nearly three million households live in "informal" housing.[22]

As Gibson goes on to note, "Their demands were far from revolutionary; they were the demands of loyal citizens making reasonable requests, borne of their citizenship, for inclusion in the 'new South Africa': for

---

19. Gibson, *Fanonian Practices in South Africa*, 144.

20. Gibson uses this phrase and I have heard it used by a representative of Abahlali who has worked with the Ujamaa Centre on a common project; Gibson, *Fanonian Practices in South Africa*, 146.

21. Patel, "Cities without Citizens."

22. Gibson, *Fanonian Practices in South Africa*, 147–48.

housing, safety, health care, and political representation."[23] And, he could have added, for respect and dignity. This addition is central to how Abahlali conceives their own struggle. What makes Abahlali distinctive among the many similar "service delivery" protests that are a feature of our twenty-year old democracy is their remarkable capacity for self-reflection. They inhabit the praxis cycle, where action leads to reflection leads to action leads to reflection, in an ongoing cycle. I am sure that the praxis cycle is a part of many of the "service delivery" protests, but what Abahlali has offered to us all is a self-conscious and structured set of action-related reflections. This becomes clear in any meeting with Abahlali representatives or in visiting their website.[24]

Speaking for themselves, as they prefer, their first president S'bu Zikode reflects on the need for shared leadership in the movement so that there is time for family and time for reflection on their "living politics." This lived politics, he argues, is "a politics that was always based on thinking carefully about lives and struggles. We have to change ourselves before we can change the world and, without time to think, that change becomes difficult."[25] Zikode's logic is clear: what they are struggling for is rooted in their relationships, to their families and to each other; and to retain this fundamental commitment and to orient their struggle around this core commitment they must make the time to reflect on their lived politics. "The struggle" is both a struggle "against" as well as a struggle "for," with the latter being emphasized by Abahlali.

This is an important recognition in our contemporary context. Our "struggle," and this became a technical, theory- and theology-laden term in the 1980s,[26] was "against" apartheid. Since 1994 our struggle has been "for," though what ought to follow this "for" has been contested, particularly in economic terms.[27] Abahlali fills this "for" with both content and process. For Abahlali, the struggle "for" is more than a struggle for the vote; it is a struggle for the meaning of the vote.[28] "For them," says Gibson, "democ-

---

23. Gibson, *Fanonian Practices in South Africa*, 148.

24. See http://www.abahlali.org, especially their "University of Abahlali baseMjondolo" page. Much of the material that Gibson uses can be found here in its original form.

25. Cited in Gibson, *Fanonian Practices in South Africa*, 154–55.

26. Nolan, *God in South Africa*; Mosala, *Biblical Hermeneutics and Black Theology*.

27. Terreblanche, *A History of Inequality in South Africa*; Saul, *The Next Liberation Struggle*.

28. Gibson, *Fanonian Practices in South Africa*, 157.

racy was not about an election every five years, but about day-to-day life that included reciprocity, caring and the inclusion of those who had been systematically excluded and told they were too stupid to understand."[29] In the words of Zikode, "(O)ur struggle is for moral questions, as compared to the political questions as such. It is more about justice. Is it good for shack dwellers to live in mud like pigs, as they are living?" he asks by way of illustration. "Why do I live in a cardboard house if there are people who are able to live in a decent house? So it is a moral question."[30] It is for this reason that Abahlali has consistently refuted the discourse of "service delivery"; "they insist instead that their demands are about 'being human'"; indeed, in the words of Zikode, "the struggle is the human being."[31] In Gibson's language, which resonates with Horsley's analysis of Q, "Abahlalism is a culture of sharing that is rooted in the ideas of community and reciprocity found in the long struggle against apartheid."[32]

It is not surprising, therefore, that notions of "dignity" have assumed such a central place in the discourse of Abahlali. "We fought, died and voted for this government," says Zikode, "so that we could be free and have decent lives."[33] One of the major goals of Abahlali, argues Gibson, building on Zikode's analysis, "is a kind of moral revolution, the creation of a society where the poor will be treated as human beings with minds of their own." As Zikode likes to say, "We are poor in life, not in mind."[34]

Yet, as Gibson goes on to note, Abahlali is regularly reminded "that poor people in post-apartheid South Africa are not valued as much as others, and while Abahlali has successfully forced itself on to the agendas of government institutions and 'civil society', there is a constant struggle not only to keep these spaces open but through their inclusion to transform them."[35] The dignity of the poor, as human beings, is constitutive of the kind of South Africa we have struggled for, both in terms of the goals of our democracy and the processes of our democracy.

In his insightful study of the art of resistance to domination, James Scott also allocates an important role to human dignity. Indeed, Scott

29. Ibid., 156–57.
30. Cited in ibid., 157.
31. Ibid.
32. Ibid., 158.
33. Cited in ibid.
34. Ibid.
35. Ibid.

admits that he privileges "the issues of dignity and autonomy, which have typically been seen as secondary to material exploitation."[36] No matter how severe the domination—and Scott focuses on extreme forms of domination—dignity always demands a response to domination. In cases of intense and sustained surveillance by the forces of domination, dignity's expression finds its place in the hidden transcript, a discourse "of dignity, of negation, and of justice" that is articulated and elaborated in those social sites that the marginalized are able to forge and secure in the face of surveillance.[37] Like Abahlali, Scott recognizes that the poor are not poor in mind. Central to his analysis is the recognition that subordinate classes "are *less* constrained at the level of thought and ideology, since they can in secluded settings speak with comparative safety, and *more* constrained at the level of political action and struggle, where the daily exercise of power sharply limits the options available to them."[38] What political liberation has brought to South Africa is the political space for the hidden transcript to enter the public realm. And Abahlali has embraced this space, giving fulsome account of dignity's revolt to the state's "systemic neglect."[39]

DIGNITY'S REVOLT

John Holloway, like Scott and Abahlali, locates dignity at the heart of social movements of the marginalized. In the Zapatista movement in Mexico, he finds evidence of the centrality of dignity. In an article posted on the Abahlali website, Holloway cites as an example a 1994 letter from the ruling body of the Zapatistas, the Comité Clandestino Revolucionario Indígena (CCRI), addressed to another indigenous organization, the Consejo 500 Años de Resistencia Indígena:

> Then that suffering that united us made us speak, and we recognized that in our words there was truth, we knew that not only pain and suffering lived in our tongue, we recognized that there is hope still in our hearts. We spoke with ourselves, we looked inside ourselves and we looked at our history: we saw our most ancient fathers suffering and struggling, we saw our grandfathers struggling, we saw our fathers with fury in their hands, we saw that not

36. Scott, *Domination and the Arts of Resistance*, xi.

37. Ibid., 114.

38. Ibid., 91.

39. Terreblanche, *A History of Inequality in South Africa*, 423.

everything had been taken away from us, that we had the most valuable, that which made us live, that which made our step rise above plants and animals, that which made the stone be beneath our feet, and we saw, brothers, that all that we had was DIGNITY, and we saw that great was the shame of having forgotten it, and we saw that DIGNITY was good for men to be men again, and dignity returned to live in our hearts, and we were new again, and the dead, our dead, saw that we were new again and they called us again, to dignity, to struggle.[40]

Holloway goes on to extract this movement's understanding of dignity from their struggle and to begin to map a political discourse that has dignity as its core. Beginning with the self-evident assertion that dignity is "the refusal to accept humiliation and dehumanization," he interrogates both the "is" and the "is not" of dignity.

Dignity, understood as a category of struggle, is a tension which points beyond itself. The assertion of dignity implies the present negation of dignity. Dignity, then, is the struggle against the denial of dignity, the struggle for the realization of dignity. Dignity is and is not: it is the struggle against its own negation. If dignity were simply the assertion of something that already is, then it would be an absolutely flabby concept, an empty complacency. To simply assert human dignity as a principle (as in "all humans have dignity," or "all humans have a right to dignity") would be either so general as to be meaningless or, worse, so general as to obscure the fact that existing society is based on the negation of dignity. Similarly, if dignity were simply the assertion of something that is not, then it would be an empty daydream or a religious wish. The concept of dignity only gains force if it is understood in its double dimension, as the struggle against its own denial.[41]

Profoundly and succinctly, "Dignity is the cry of 'here we are!'" Holloway goes on to pursue both the moral and political dimensions of this assertion.

Dignity is an assault on the separation of morality and politics, and of the private and the public. Dignity cuts across those boundaries, asserts the unity of what has been sundered. The assertion of dignity is neither a moral nor a political claim: it is rather an attack on the separation of politics and morality that allows

40. http://l`ibcom.org/library/dignitys-revolt-john-holloway
41. Ibid.

formally democratic regimes all over the world to co-exist with growing levels of poverty and social marginalization. It is the "here we are!" not just of the marginalized, but of the horror felt by all of us in the face of mass impoverishment and starvation. It is the "here we are!" not just of the growing numbers shut away in prisons, hospitals and homes, but also of the shame and disgust of all of us who, by living, participate in the bricking up of people in those prisons, hospitals and homes. Dignity is an assault on the conventional definition of politics, but equally on the acceptance of that definition in the instrumental conception of revolutionary politics which has for so long subordinated the personal to the political, with such disastrous results.[42]

Dignity encapsulates, says Holloway, "in one word the rejection of the separation of the personal and the political," and the revolt of dignity "derives its strength from the uniting of dignities. . . . Dignity resonates. As it vibrates, it sets off vibrations in other dignities, an unstructured, possibly discordant resonance."[43]

Reading through the diverse genres of discourse on the Abahlali website, one finds similar sentiments, organically related to their own particular struggle. For example, Abahlali leader Lindela Figlan offers a detailed reflection on the contours of dignity from their perspective.[44] He begins by dealing with what dignity is not, saying:

[T]he meaning of dignity is often misunderstood. Many people only think of dignity in relation to the economic status of those who are better off. This is understood to mean that a person with no money is taken as a person whose life and voice does not count and is therefore a person with no dignity. It is also understood that a person with money does count and is therefore a person with dignity. But no amount of money can buy dignity.

While money may buy many things,

---

42. Ibid.

43. http://libcom.org/library/dignitys-revolt-john-holloway. I have chosen to cite this article in the form in which it is represented on the Abahlali website, as part of the "University of Abahlali baseMjondolo." The article has been published as Holloway, "Dignity's Revolt." Scott uses a similar image in *Domination and the Arts of Resistance*, 224.

44. http://abahlali.org/node/9325. All quotations that follow are from this URL. The extensive citation here is deliberate, offering us an encounter with the internal emic logic of Abahlali's conception of dignity.

money does not buy dignity because to be a person with dignity you must recognize the dignity of others. No person is a complete person on their own, that is without others. In isiZulu we say "umuntu ungumuntu ngabantu" ("a person is a person because of other people").

In sum, "there is dignity in respecting the humanity of others and in being respected back."

Figlan then turns specifically to the conditions that mitigate against dignity.

As poor people we do not live in dignified conditions. In fact when it rains we live like pigs in the mud. Our shacks are always burning. We do not have toilets. We are disrespected by politicians and, when we have work, we are disrespected at work. Security guards and domestic workers are often treated as if we are not fully human.

Significantly, Figlan singles out people like us, scholars, as another sector that disrespects the poor. "Sometimes," he says, "we are also disrespected by NGOs, academics and other people that think that they have a right to lead the struggles of the poor and who get very angry when we explain that for us solidarity must be based on talking to us and not for us and thinking and deciding with us and not for us."

Figlan insists on the agency of the poor: "But poor as we are we achieve our own dignity." He then goes on to enumerate the variety of sites in which dignity is achieved, saying that "some people achieve dignity in their churches. Some achieve dignity through culture, in something like a choir." Fundamentally, however, he says, "we achieve dignity in the togetherness of our struggle. Our struggle is a space of dignity. Here we can express our suffering, we can think together and we can support each other."[45]

Reminding his listeners that he is speaking from a postliberation context, Figlan says, "[T]he rights that we have on paper were always refused in reality. This included our rights as citizens, our rights to the cities and our rights to respect and dignity." Locating dignity at the nexus of this refusal, Figlan goes on to say,

Whenever we asked for our rights to be respected, for our humanity to be recognized, we were presented as troublemakers, as people that were being used by others, or as criminals. Our request

45. Ibid.

to participate in the discussions about our own lives was taken as a threat. It is important that everyone understands that in this regard civil society and the left was often no different to the state.

But over against the state, civil society, and the left, "Abahlali has been organizing and mobilizing to build the power of the poor from below." But Figlan is not referring here to the organizing of "others." "We do not organise people," he says. "We organise ourselves."[46]

Figlan then goes on to address the position of Abahlali with respect to politics. "We do not support any political parties or vote in elections," he says. The reason is twofold. First, "politicians are always using the people's suffering and struggles as ladders to build their own power." And second, "we have therefore decided that we will not keep on giving our power away. We build our own power in our communities and encourage people to also build their own power where they work, study and pray. Where possible we govern our own communities ourselves."[47]

The core problem, Figlan argues, is that "we have learnt that this order is one that cannot respect our humanity. In fact this order is based on our exploitation and exclusion. This order is designed to oppress us. Therefore we have understood that, as Mnikelo Ndabankulu first said, it is good to be out of order. We are not loyal to this order." But this turn "from" entails a turn "to." "We are loyal to our human dignity and to the human dignity of others and when that requires us to be out of order we are prepared to be out of order." Human dignity is the fulcrum or pivot of the movement's identity.[48]

By identifying the agency of "the organized poor" Figlan reminds theologians of the notion of "the epistemological privilege of the poor,"[49] which was central to liberation theology. Though not engaging with this trajectory explicitly, Figlan goes on to enunciate clearly what this notion implies. "As repression gets worse," Figlan says, "solidarity becomes more and more important." But he is clear that respect for Abahlali's autonomy is vital to any meaningful solidarity. S'bu Zikode reiterates this stance on solidarity, placing dignity at the center of their call for solidarity, saying, "The dignity of the poor is the starting point of our politics and it must

46. Ibid.

47. Ibid.

48. Ibid.

49. For a fuller discussion see Frostin, "The Hermeneutics of the Poor"; Frostin, *Liberation Theology in Tanzania and South Africa*.

also be the starting point of any living solidarity with our struggles. . . . Talk with and not for us. Think with and not for us. Plan with us and not for us."[50]

Dignity is agentive; dignity is more a verb than a noun. In the words of a joint statement by Abahlali baseMjondolo, the Rural Network, and the Unemployed People's Movement, "Dignity is the road and it is the destination."[51]

PEOPLE'S THEOLOGY

I have quoted Abahlali at length because they represent a call to socially engaged biblical scholars and theologians to enter into solidarity with them and to do theology with them. The Revised Second Edition (1986) of the *Kairos Document* prepares the way for us, making a distinction between "people's theology" and "prophetic theology."

> It should also be noted that there is a subtle difference between prophetic theology and people's theology. The Kairos Document itself, signed by theologians, ministers and other church workers, and addressed to all who bear the name Christian is a prophetic statement. But the process that led to the production of the document, the process of theological reflection and action in groups, the involvement of many different people in doing theology was an exercise in people's theology. The document is therefore pointing out two things: that our present Kairos challenges Church leaders and other Christians to speak out prophetically and that our present Kairos is challenging all of us to do theology together reflecting upon our experiences in working for justice and peace in South Africa and thereby developing a better theological understanding of our Kairos. The method that was used to produce the Kairos Document shows that theology is not the preserve of professional theologians, ministers and priests. Ordinary Christians can participate in theological reflection and should be encouraged to do so. When this people's theology is proclaimed to others to challenge and inspire them, it takes on the character of a prophetic theology.[52]

There can be no prophetic theology without there first being a people's theology, according to the *Kairos Document*. This is an important and timely reminder as some are attempting to revive "kairos theology" in

50. http://abahlali.org/node/9753

51. http://abahlali.org/node/9478

52. *The Kairos Document*, 34–35, note 15; Leonard, 63, note 15.

South Africa,[53] but without organic links to people's movements. A prophetic theological praxis that was rooted in people's theology is a distinctive feature of the strand of South African theology that came to be called "contextual theology," and the *Kairos Document* is perhaps the best example of this praxis.[54] Sadly, however, this legacy has been neglected since our political liberation. But as Abahlali reminds us, the need has not diminished; it simply has a different face. And the resources remain. The Institute for Contextual Theology (ICT) and the work of Albert Nolan have been instrumental in both theorizing and facilitating this people's theology/prophetic theology process of doing theology.[55] So there is a guiding methodology for doing theology "with" social movements within the kind of solidarity envisaged by Abahlali, if we are prepared to heed the call. The "raw material" is already there; people's theology is already present in the dignity discourse of Abahlali.

If we return to the inaugural protests that gave birth to Abahlali base-Mjondolo, people's theology was present. In welcoming the fourteen who had been arrested by the police and held for ten days,

> Zikode, together with Nonhlanhla Mzombe and other community activists, organized a welcome home party for the fourteen, at which Zikode held the crowd rapt with the following affirmation of their actions. "The first Nelson Mandela," he explained, "was Jesus Christ. The second was Nelson Rolihlahla Mandela. The third Nelson Mandela are the poor people of the world."[56]

Reflecting on this people's theology, Nigel Gibson offers a further (though non-theological) articulation, saying:

> The resonance was clear. The poor weren't Christ, but Christ was the first Mandela, the first liberator who articulated a new heaven and a new earth. Mandela is Christ reborn, grounding liberation firmly on South African soil, his long imprisonment during apartheid a metaphor for the nation, just as his release is identified with the birth of a new South Africa. Yet, the failure of the historical

53. See the "Kairos Southern Africa" initiative: http://kairossouthernafrica.wordpress.com/.

54. West, "Liberation Hermeneutics after Liberation in South Africa"; West, "The Legacy of Liberation Theologies in South Africa."

55. Nolan, "Kairos Theology"; Nolan, "Work, the Bible, Workers, and Theologians"; Cochrane, "Questioning Contextual Theology."

56. http://abahlali.org/node/302

Mandela to liberate South Africa demanded the birth of a new Mandela: the poor themselves. After many promises, all of them broken, they saw through the rhetoric of the local authorities. Enough was enough—*sekwanele, sekwanele!*—truth emanated from their own experiences: they had become the "new reality of the nation," declaring the shack dwellers' movement a university where they "think their own struggles" and "are not poor in mind."[57] Subtly criticizing Mandela's historical leadership, the poor were taking matters into their own hands, seeing themselves as the force and reason for their own liberation; they had become their own Mandelas.[58]

Those of us who are theologians could take this further, for surely S'bu Zikode is saying that Mandela comes/stands in the trajectory of Jesus Christ. He is, in some respects, like Christ. But the real Mandela, the second Mandela has not been fully faithful to this prophetic trajectory,[59] and so another has arisen in the prophetic trajectory of Jesus: the people themselves. Put differently, from the perspective of a biblical scholar, the people (in Abahlali's particular sense of the term) were always at the core of God's project of liberation, with their own organic intellectuals, like Jesus, who gave prophetic expression to the people's theology of each particular era. God's project was always about the people, with the people as the key agents of the project, with God.

DIGNITY AFTER MANDELA

In its initial tribute to Nelson Mandela on his death (December 5, 2013), the African National Congress offered its own theological commentary, saying, "He loved the ANC. Hence his frequent words that upon his death he would join 'the nearest branch of the ANC in heaven.'"[60] This is perhaps an allusion to the theological notion expressed in The Lord's Prayer, where Jesus (through Q and Matthew) reminds his disciples that they should pray for God's kingdom to come on earth "as it is in heaven" (Matt 6:10). And in his tribute to Mandela, which emphasizes the theological dimensions of

57. Citing Zikode, "'We Are the Third Force.'"

58. Gibson, *Fanonian Practices in South Africa*, 147.

59. I invoke here Walter Brueggemann's sense of "trajectory"; see Brueggemann, "Trajectories in Old Testament Literature and the Sociology of Ancient Israel."

60. http://mg.co.za/article/2013-12-06-anc-remembers-mandela-as-large-african-boabab.

Mandela's legacy, Anthony Egan draws attention to the centrality of dignity. In his theological tribute to Nelson Mandela, Anthony Egan, from the Jesuit Institute of South Africa, locates dignity at the center of Mandela's theological legacy. He "lived dignity" and he "demanded" dignity, says Egan.[61]

While we cannot dispute Mandela's personal legacy, Abahlali demands that this legacy take structural form. The weave of the fabric of our society, they claim, must be constituted by dignity. Sampie Terreblanche reminds us that South Africa has inherited "a history of inequality." South Africa's economic system has moved, Terreblanche argues, "over the past 30 years from one of colonial and racial capitalism to a neo-liberal, first-world, capitalist enclave that is disengaging itself from a large part of the black labour force." This transformation, he continues, though it has "coincided with the introduction of a system of representative democracy which is effectively controlled by a black, predominantly African, elite," still exhibits "an ominous systemic character."

> In the new politico-economic system, individual members of the upper classes (comprising one third of the population) profit handsomely from mainstream economic activity, while the mainly black lumpenproletariat (comprising 50 per cent of the population) is increasingly pauperised. Ironically, individual members of the black and white upper class in the new system seem as unconcerned about its dysfunctionality as individual members of the white elite were about that of the old. The common denominator between the old and the new systems is that part of society was/is systemically and undeservedly enriched, while the majority of the population were/are systemically and undeservedly impoverished—in the old system through *systemic exploitation*, and in the new system through *systemic neglect*.[62]

Abahlali locates the center of this systemic neglect in the refusal to recognize the dignity of the poor and marginalized. And it is the argument of this essay that the biblical and theological project of socially engaged scholars includes locating ourselves and our resources alongside such social movements. Among the resources we can offer are the tools to recognize the dignity of marginal voices in our biblical and theological traditions. That our biblical and theological traditions are internally

---

61. Egan, "Nelson Rolihlahla Mandela."

62. Terreblanche, *A History of Inequality in South Africa*, 422–23.

contested is a significant conceptual contribution in itself.[63] But if we make this claim, then we must also offer the kinds of resources that enable access to these contending voices. This point is made somewhat provocatively by Xola Skosana, a Christian minister from Cape Town. He has called prophetically for the black preacher to "exhume the black body of Jesus from the grave." "The black preacher must point to the cross and remind black people that their cross on the ballot paper on May 18, 2011 should not be to legitimise and perpetuate the corruption and political hegemony that keep black people in servitude and in modernised slavery." But, says *Mail and Guardian* writer Percy Zvomuya, having interviewed Skosana, "today's black preacher is incapable of that, Skosana believes," for "he lacks the necessary tools, skills and the gift to place scripture in its context. The black preacher is unwilling to submit 'to the discipline of study' and is given to the 'gimmicks' first sold to him by 'the American TV evangelist.'"[64]

Zvomuya is correct in saying as the headline to his article puts it, "Jesus Christ lived in the townships." He did indeed, and his people are the people represented in Q (and Mark), in the people of the *Son of Man* film, and in the people of the shack settlements, people who continue to construct their struggle around the central core of dignity. The people in their struggle are dignity's trajectory. Zvomuya is also correct in recognizing that prophetic theology requires particular tools, skills, and gifts in order to read Scripture contextually.

AN AMBIGUOUS BIBLE

The Kairos Document (1985) identified three theological trajectories within which the struggle for dignity in South Africa could be located. It argued that "state theology," the theology of the apartheid state (and its ecclesiastical alliance partners), constituted a direct attack on the dignity of certain sectors. Racial discrimination was an assault on human dignity. "Church theology," the mainstream theology of the churches, had a similar effect. By steadfastly focusing on the individual, yet refusing to locate the individual within political and economic structures, "church theology" participated in the systemic denigration of aspects of human dignity. Against these two dominant theological trajectories, the *Kairos Document* called the churches

---

63. See Anderson, *Ancient Laws and Contemporary Controversies.*
64. http://abahlali.org/node/7992.

in South Africa towards a "prophetic theology" in which human dignity was central.

However, the *Kairos Document* erred in arguing that both "state theology" and "church theology" were not biblical theologies.[65] For, unfortunately, both of these theological trajectories are found in the Bible. Indeed, this is what made them so dangerous: they are biblical theologies. And while some forms of South African theology have not had the tools to deal with this scriptural reality, South African "black theology" offers us the resources we need, via the work of Itumeleng Mosala. The Bible, according to Mosala's analysis, is a complex text best understood as a "signified practice." "It cannot be reduced to a simple socially and ideologically unmediated 'Word of God.' Nor can it be seen merely as a straight forward mirror of events in ancient Israel. On the contrary it is a *production*, a remaking of those events and processes."[66] Using the language of redaction criticism (and drawing on Robert Coote's work on Amos),[67] Mosala argues that different "layers" can be detected within or across biblical books, each with a particular ideological code. Some layers of the Bible are cast in "hegemonic codes," which represent social and historical realities in ancient Israel in terms of the interests of the ruling classes. Other parts of the Bible are encoded in "professional codes," which have a relative autonomy, but which still operate within the hegemony of the dominant code. Then there are layers that are signified through "negotiated codes," which contain a mixture of adaptive and oppositional elements, but which still take the dominant codes as their starting point. Finally, there are a few textual sites or sources that represent "oppositional codes" which are grounded in the interests and religious perspectives of the underclasses of the communities of the Bible.[68]

Similar work has been done with the New Testament, as indicated above in Horsley's analysis of the synoptic gospels. Horsley and others discern distinctive oral and textual voices in and behind the final form of the text.[69] How many layers or voices there are is not the key question; what is important, as Mosala makes clear, is recognizing that there are contending voices in Scripture. The discourse of dignity is nurtured, as both Scott and

---

65. West, "Tracing the 'Kairos' Trajectory from South Africa (1985) to Palestine (2009)."

66. Mosala, "Black Theology."

67. Coote, *Amos among the Prophets.*

68. Mosala, *Biblical Hermeneutics and Black Theology,* 41–42.

69. Horsley, *Oral Performance, Popular Tradition, and Hidden Transcript in Q.*

Horsley demonstrate, in the sites that the poor and marginalized secure in the face of domination. It is through this internal ethic that "a discourse of dignity, of negation, and of justice" is forged and fostered.[70] And it is here that the socially engaged biblical scholar is invited to offer his/her resources for working with an ambiguous Bible.

BIBLIOGRAPHY

Anderson, Cheryl B. *Ancient Laws and Contemporary Controversies: The Need for Inclusive Biblical Interpretation*. Oxford: Oxford University Press, 2009.

Brueggemann, Walter. "A Shape for Old Testament Theology, I: Structure Legitimation." In *Old Testament Theology: Essays on Structure, Theme, and Text*, edited by Patrick D. Miller, 1–21. Minneapolis: Fortress, 1992.

———. "A Shape for Old Testament Theology, II: Embrace of Pain." In *Old Testament Theology: Essays on Structure, Theme, and Text*, edited by Patrick D. Miller, 22–44. Minneapolis: Fortress, 1992.

———. "Trajectories in Old Testament Literature and the Sociology of Ancient Israel." In *The Bible and Liberation: Political and Social Hermeneutics*, edited by Norman K. Gottwald and Richard A. Horsley, 201–26. Maryknoll, NY: Orbis, 1993.

Cochrane, James R. "Questioning Contextual Theology." In *Towards an Agenda for Contextual Theology: Essays in Honour of Albert Nolan*, edited by McGlory T. Speckman and Larry T. Kaufmann, 67–86. Pietermaritzburg: Cluster, 2001.

Coote, Robert B. *Amos among the Prophets: Composition and Theology*. Philadelphia: Fortress Press, 1981.

Egan, Anthony. "Nelson Mandela: A Theological Perspective." No pages. Online: http://en.radiovaticana.va/storico/2013/12/06/nelson_mandela_a_theological_perspective/en1-753299.

Frostin, Per. "The Hermeneutics of the Poor: The Epistemological 'Break' in Third World Theologies." *Studia Theologica* 39 (1985) 127–50.

———. *Liberation Theology in Tanzania and South Africa: A First World Interpretation*. Lund: Lund University Press, 1988.

Gibson, Nigel. *Fanonian Practices in South Africa: From Steve Biko to Abahlali Basemjondolo*. New York: Palgrave Macmillan, 2011.

Gottwald, Norman K. *The Hebrew Bible: A Socio-Literary Introduction*. Philadelphia: Fortress, 1985.

———. *The Tribes of Yahweh: A Sociology of the Religion of Liberated Israel, 1250–1050 B.C.* Maryknoll, NY: Orbis, 1979.

Holloway, John. "Dignity's Revolt." In *Zapatista! Reinventing Revolution in Mexico*, edited by John Holloway and Elíona Peláez, 159–98. London: Pluto, 1998.

Horsley, Richard A. *Oral Performance, Popular Tradition, and Hidden Transcript in Q*. Semeia Studies 60. Atlanta: Society of Biblical Literature, 2006.

———. *Sociology and the Jesus Movement*. 2nd ed. New York: Continuum, 1994.

Kairos Document. *Challenge to the Church: The Kairos Document: A Theological Comment on the Political Crisis in South Africa*. Braamfontein: The Kairos theologians, 1985.

70. Scott, *Domination and the Arts of Resistance*, 114.

————. *Challenge to the Church: A Theological Comment on the Political Crisis in South Africa*. 2nd ed. Braamfontein: Skotaville, 1986.

Leonard, Gary S. D. *Kairos: The Moment of Truth. "The Time Has Come. The Moment of Truth Has Arrived."* Pietermaritzburg: Ujamaa Centre, 2011.

Maluleke, Tinyiko S. "Black Theology as Public Discourse." In *Constructing a Language of Religion in Public Life: Multi-Event 1999 Academic Workshop Papers*, edited by James R. Cochrane, 60–62. Cape Town: University of Cape Town, 1998.

Mosala, Itumeleng J. *Biblical Hermeneutics and Black Theology in South Africa*. Grand Rapids: Eerdmans, 1989.

————. "Black Theology." Unpublished paper, 1989.

Nolan, Albert. *God in South Africa: The Challenge of the Gospel*. Cape Town: David Philip, 1988.

————. "Kairos Theology." In *Doing Theology in Context: South African Perspectives*, edited by John W. de Gruchy and Charles Villa-Vicencio, 212–18. Cape Town: David Philip, 1994.

————. "Work, the Bible, Workers, and Theologians: Elements of a Workers' Theology." *Semeia* 73 (1996) 213–20.

Patel, Raj. "Cities without Citizens: A Perspective on the Struggle of Abahlali Basemjondolo, the Durban Shackdweller Movement." In *Contesting Development: Critical Struggles for Social Change*, edited by Philip McMichael, 33–49. London: Routledge, 2009.

Saul, John S. *The Next Liberation Struggle: Capitalism, Socialism and Democracy in Southern Africa*. Pietermaritzburg: University of KwaZulu-Natal Press, 2005.

Scott, James C. *Domination and the Arts of Resistance: Hidden Transcripts*. New Haven: Yale University Press, 1990.

Son of Man. Directed by Mark Dornford-May. Produced by Dimpho di Kopane, 2006.

Terreblanche, Sampie. *A History of Inequality in South Africa, 1652–2002*. Pietermaritzburg: University of Natal Press, 2002.

West, Gerald O. "The Legacy of Liberation Theologies in South Africa, with an Emphasis on Biblical Hermeneutics." *Studia Historiae Ecclesiasticae* 63 (July 2010) 157–83.

————. "Liberation Hermeneutics after Liberation in South Africa." In *The Bible and the Hermeneutics of Liberation*, edited by Alejandro F. Botta and P. R. Andiñach, 13–38. Atlanta: Society of Biblical Literature, 2009.

————. "The Son of Man in South Africa?" In *Son of Man: An African Jesus Film*, edited by Richard Walsh, Jeffrey L. Staley, and Adele Reinhartz, 2–22. Sheffield, UK: Sheffield Phoenix, 2013.

————. "Tracing the 'Kairos' Trajectory from South Africa (1985) to Palestine (2009): Discerning Continuities and Differences." *Journal of Theology for Southern Africa* 143 (2012) 4–22.

Zikode, S'bu. "'The Third Force.'" *Journal of Asian and African Studies* 41/1–2 (2006) 185–89.

PART 4

Xenophobia

6

The Strangers in the Second Half of Leviticus

Esias E. Meyer,
Faculty of Theology, University of Pretoria

INTRODUCTION

TEN YEARS AGO I followed Christiana van Houten in her interpretation that the *gērim* in the Holiness Code were the Judean people who remained behind during the exile.[1] The struggle between the Israelites and the *gērim* depicted in these texts was thus actually an inner-Judean power struggle between those who returned from exile and those who never left. The former understood themselves as representing the true Israel, while the latter also considered themselves as belonging to Israel, but as having lost the power struggle in the Persian province of Yehud. This kind of interpretation is obviously not very conducive to a restorative reading of these texts, but actually makes the texts seem rather dark and very oppressive. They become examples of what we as modern-day Christians should not be or do. My reasons for following Van Houten had to do with the approach I

1. Meyer, *Jubilee*, 244–52; Van Houten, *Alien*, 140–55.

had chosen in my engagement with Leviticus 25.[2] Actually, Van Houten's interpretation has since been rejected by most other scholars. The fact that scholars such as Jacob Milgrom and Christophe Nihan, whose work I will be engaging later, have rejected her interpretation has also encouraged me to relinquish this particular interpretation and follow a more traditional view of the *gēr*.[3] According to this view, the *gēr* is someone who comes from outside Israel or Judah and eventually settles there. The following essay is then an attempt to once again engage with the issue of the *gērim* or strangers in the book of Leviticus. The essay will start by providing an overview of the occurrences of the term in Leviticus and will then attempt to describe the current state of the debate by looking at the recent contributions of both Milgrom and Nihan. In both cases a critical evaluation will be offered, also in the light of other recent contributions. The essay asks whether we can learn anything from how the authors of the book of Leviticus thought that they and their addressees should treat the strangers in their midst. The answer is a rather surprising "yes." The noun *gēr* appears twenty-one times[4] in the second half of Leviticus. The first occurrence is in chapter 16 at the end of the chapter on the Day of Atonement and the last example is found at the end of chapter 25. One also finds the verb *gwr* (usually as a participle) eleven times[5] in Leviticus. In nine[6] of these instances the *gēr* is the subject of the verb *gwr* and on two other occasions the subject is either the *tôšāb* (Lev 25:24) or a whole list of different social groups including the *tôšāb*, but excluding the *gēr* (Lev 25:6). Since we will refer again to the *tôšāb* later, it is worth noting that this term is found eight times[7] in Leviticus, of which seven are in chapter 25.[8] I will offer a brief overview of the contents of these different examples. Apart from one exception (Lev 16:29), all of these examples are found in what has traditionally been called the Holiness Code which consists of Leviticus 17–26. With regard to the

2. See Meyer, *Jubilee*, 11–64. I followed Robert Carroll and his approach of *Ideologiekritik* which is an approach highly conscious of power and ideology in the biblical text, but also in the context of the interpreter.

3. Milgrom, *Leviticus 17–22*, 1500; Nihan, "Resident Aliens," 114.

4. See Lev 16:29; 17:8, 10, 12, 13, 15; 18:26; 19:10, 33, 34 (x2); 20:2; 22:18; 23:22; 24:16, 22; 25:, 23, 35, 47 (x3).

5. See Lev 16:29; 17:8, 10, 12, 13; 18:26; 19:33, 34; 20:2; 25:6, 45.

6. See Lev 16:29; 17:8, 10, 12, 13; 18:26; 19:33, 34; 20:2.

7. See Lev 22:10; 25:6, 23, 35, 40, 45, 47 (x2).

8. As Rendtorff points out, the term only occurs fourteen times in the whole Hebrew Bible and half of these are in Leviticus 25. Rendtorff, "The *gēr*," 79.

Holiness Code, there seems to be an emerging consensus that it is what we would call a post-priestly document, meaning that it was written after the Priestly text (P). This has been argued by Jewish scholars such as Milgrom[9] and Knohl,[10] with many European[11] scholars in agreement with them; although most scholars[12] do not agree with the preexilic dating offered by Milgrom and Knohl. With regard to the Holiness Code, a lot of work done in Europe also builds on studies by earlier German scholars such as Karl Elliger[13] and Alfred Cholewinksi.[14] More and more scholars are also arguing that H[15] is much broader than just Leviticus 17–26. Texts in Leviticus which are usually regarded as part of H are Lev 11:43–45 and 16:29–34a.[16] Arguments in support of this contention are usually based on the language. Thus, Lev 11:43–45 has the language of "holiness" in common with the parenetic frame of the Holiness Code.[17] Leviticus 16:29–34a has, amongst other things, the concern for the *gēr* in common with the rest of H in the second half of Leviticus.[18]

OVERVIEW OF TEXTS REFERRING TO THE GĒRIM

In Lev 16:29, after the description of the Day of Atonement, one reads:

9. See especially Milgrom, *Leviticus 17–22*, 1361–64.

10. Knohl, *Sanctuary*.

11. See, for instance, Otto, "Innerbiblische Exegese," 125–96. Nihan, *Priestly Torah*.

12. There are some European scholars who would also follow Kauffman in terms of dating P as preexilic. Two examples which we will engage with later are Zehnder, *Umgang*, 323; and Joosten, *People and Land*, 9–15.

13. Elliger, *Leviticus*.

14. Cholewinski, *Heiligkeitsgesetz*.

15. The Holiness Code is often abbreviated to "H." In this essay, H will refer not only to the Holiness Code (Lev 17–26), but will include other texts in the Pentateuch often associated with the Holiness Code.

16. I include these two texts since they will be mentioned later in this essay. For both Milgrom and Knohl, H is of course much broader and includes texts from Exodus, Numbers, and the first half of Leviticus. See Milgrom, *Leviticus 17–22*, 1332–44, where he also discusses the work of Knohl. For a critique of Knohl, see Nihan, *Priestly Torah*, 564–72, whose H is much more modest than Knohl's. Nihan also includes Leviticus 11:43–45 and 16:29–34a.

17. See Milgrom, *Leviticus 1–16*, 694–96. For a discussion of the parenetic frame of the Holiness Code see Otto, "Innerbiblische Exegese," 172–76.

18. See Nihan, *Priestly Torah*, 347–50 and 569, or Milgrom, *Leviticus 1–16*, 1064–65.

> This shall be a statute to you forever: In the seventh month, on the
> tenth day of the month, you shall deny yourselves, and shall do
> no work, neither the citizen nor the alien who resides among you
> (Lev 16:29 NRSV).

The same obligations are laid on the *gēr* as on the *'ĕzrāḥ* (citizen) in
Leviticus 16. The next chapter which is traditionally regarded as the start of
the Holiness Code, Leviticus 17, has five occurrences of the noun *gēr*. In all
five cases one reads of further obligations which the *gēr* must honor. Verse
8 forbids them to sacrifice at any other place than the entrance of the tent of
meeting. The rest of the chapter is about blood and in verses 10 and 12 the
gērim are forbidden along with the Israelites[19] to eat blood. In verse 13 they
are commanded to pour out the blood of a hunted animal and cover it with
dust, just as Israelites do. In verse 15 a ritual of purification is described for
the *gēr* or the *'ĕzrāḥ* who has eaten wild animals that have died naturally.
Leviticus 18:26 lays a further obligation on the *gēr* along with the *'ĕzrāḥ*
when they are commanded at the end of the chapter not to commit any of
the taboos mentioned (various sexual taboos). It is thus clear that the occurrences in Leviticus 16 to 18 are all about things which the *gērim* must or
must not do and they are always applied to the Israelite addressees as well,
or it would be more precise to say that the *gērim* are included when these
obligations are imposed on the Israelite addressees. The Israelite addressees
are either referred to as being an *'ĕzrāḥ*,[20] or a more collective term for the
Israelites[21] is used. This brings us to chapter 19, which is not about obligations any longer. Chapter 19 is probably the most varied chapter in all of H,
with a strange mixture of apodictic laws, some of which remind us of the
Decalogue.[22] In both cases where the *gērim* are mentioned in Leviticus 19
the addressees are commanded to do something to the *gērim*—something
good. Verse 10 says:

> You shall not strip your vineyard bare, or gather the fallen grapes
> of your vineyard; you shall leave them for the poor and the alien: I
> am the Lord your God (Lev 19:10 NRSV).

19. In verse 10 the text refers to the "house of Israel" and in verses 12 and 13 to the
"sons of Israel."

20. Lev 16:29; 17:15; 18:26; 24:16, 22.

21. Lev 17:8, 10, 12, 13; 20:2; 22:18.

22. See, for instance, Balentine, *Torah's Vision*, 169–71.

The *gērim* are thus seen as part of the poor—people in need—or the *personae miserae*, as they are often called. Verses 33–34 take this to a slightly different level.

> When an alien resides with you in your land, you shall not oppress the alien. The alien who resides with you shall be to you as the citizen among you; you shall love the alien as yourself, for you were aliens in the land of Egypt: I am the Lord your God (Lev 19:33–34 NRSV).

The addressees are commanded not to oppress the poor in verse 33, and in verse 34 they are expected to treat the *gēr* as they would a fellow Israelite. They are then asked to love the *gēr* as themselves, which resonates with what was previously said in verse 18, where the addressees are commanded to love their neighbors as themselves. This is also the first occurrence of the addressees being reminded of the fact that they themselves were *gērim* when they were in Egypt. In Lev 20:2 we find an example closer to earlier ones (chapters 16–18) where the *gērim* are forbidden, like the Israelites to give their offspring to Molech. The same goes for 22:18 where the *gērim* and the Israelites are commanded to sacrifice only animals without blemish. In both cases the *gērim* are included in commands given to the addressees. In the next example (Lev 23:22) we are again reminded of Leviticus 19:10. The addressees may not harvest the edges of their field, but must leave them for the *gērim* and the poor.

Leviticus 24:16 and 22 once again place similar obligations on the *'ĕzrāḥ* and the *gēr* by stating that both will be ruled by the same law, which in this case means not to curse God. The last five examples are all found in Leviticus 25. Verse 23 is probably the best known verse in this chapter:

> The land shall not be sold in perpetuity, for the land is mine; with me you are but aliens and tenants (Lev 25:23 NRSV).

This verse acts like a hinge in the middle of the chapter and for the second time (as in 19:34) the addressees are addressed as *gērim*, now also as *tôšābim* who are "with" YHWH. The last examples are limited to the second and fourth "case" described in the second half of Leviticus 25.[23] Verse 35 engages with the problem of a fellow Israelite falling into debt and becoming the debt slave of another Israelite. Yet he may not be taken advantage of, but should rather be treated like a *gēr* or *tôšāb*, the same terms used to describe

---

23. For a more detailed discussion of the four cases in the second part of Leviticus 25, see Meyer, *Jubilee*, 130–43.

the addressees' relationship with YHWH in verse 23. In the fourth case in verse 47, we hear of a poor "brother" ending up with a rich *gēr* and what needs to be done to get the fellow Israelite out of the claws of the stranger. The noun *gēr* is used three times, twice paired with *tôšāb*. I have left out one further important example so far, which was the single case where *tôšāb* was the subject of the verb *gwr*, found in verse 45, which belongs to the third case in the second half of Leviticus 25. This verse allows Israelites to enslave the *tôšābim* who are residing in their midst. Apart from this last example mentioned in 25:45,[24] scholars have mostly interpreted these laws applicable to the *gērim* as positive. The two cases in chapters 19 and 23, where they are mentioned with the poor, and ask the addressees to take care of them are similar to other examples one finds in the Covenant Code and the Deuteronomic Code.[25] Yet some commentators have been especially impressed with all the examples where the *gērim* were included in commandments addressed to the Israelites.[26] Others have even argued that what we see here is an earlier version of what later became the proselytes of the intertestamental period.[27] Some saw in these laws a kind of opening up towards the strangers in a society that was slowly starting to include others instead of excluding them.[28] One dissenting voice to this kind of argumentation was the late Jacob Milgrom, who had a different understanding of these laws.

MILGROM

Milgrom's argument was simply that all the laws including the *gērim* were not acts of inclusion, but more pragmatic acts that acknowledged the

24. See, Gerstenberger, *Das 3. Buch*, 357, who thinks that there is an "eklatanter Widerspruch" between Leviticus 25:45 and other texts concerning the *gērim* in the rest of Leviticus. One should keep in mind that this verse is actually about the *tôšābim* and not the *gērim*. It will become clear later that these two groups are not exactly the same. Gerstenberger regarded them as the same and then there is a clear "contradiction."

25. See the overview provided by Achenbach, "gēr," 30–32. Or Albertz, "From Aliens," 54–56.

26. See for instance, Sparks, *Ethnicity*, 251–53, who refers to the *gēr* as an "assimilated foreigner" who is part of the "religious community." Sparks also thinks that the word *gēr* was already "becoming synonymous with our word 'proselyte.'"

27. See Nihan, "Resident Aliens," 114, where he discusses scholars such as Bertholet, Baentsch, Elliger, Kellerman, etc.; or see Ramírez Kidd, *Alterity*, 49–51.

28. See Gerstenberger, *Israel in der Perserzeit*, 385, who in the light of the above-mentioned texts from H would argue that there were "starke Kräfte in der Gemeinde die volle Integration von Fremden aus theologischen Gründen wollten" (strong powers in the congregation that wanted full integration of foreigners on theological grounds).

presence of the *gērim*, but also indicated fear that their very presence might bedevil the relationship of Israel with the land and YHWH.[29] For Milgrom, the *gēr* is included in what he calls "prohibitive commandments."[30] The rationale behind this inclusion is an attempt to eliminate impurity which threatens God's land and sanctuary. Milgrom puts it as follows:

> It therefore makes no difference whether the polluter is Israelite or non-Israelite. Anyone in residence on YHWH's land is capable of polluting it or his sanctuary.[31]

The prohibitive commandments are thus the ones in which the *gēr* is included, such as not working on the Day of Atonement, not eating blood, not violating the sexual taboos of chapter 18, not sacrificing your children to Molech (chapter 20), and not sacrificing blemished animals (chapter 23) to YHWH. Milgrom contrasts these with "performative commandments," which are violations of omission, which are never addressed to the *gēr*.[32] Milgrom sums it up as follows:

> In sum, the *gēr* was expected to observe all the prohibitive commandments, lest their violation lead to the pollution of God's sanctuary and land, which, in turn, results in God's alienation and Israel's exile.[33]

Thus the implication of Milgrom's argument is that the laws mentioned above are not aimed at including the *gērim* into Israel, they are simply attempts to protect Israel from losing its land. Many scholars have followed this explanation offered by Milgrom, but as far as I can see his explanation leaves three aspects of the description of the *gēr* unexplained: The *first* has to do with Lev 19:10 and 23:22, where the *gēr* is associated with the poor and the addressees are commanded to leave something of the harvest for them. On the face of it, these texts are not about protecting the land from the impurities of the *gērim*. These texts also have a lot in common with how the *gērim* are portrayed in the other two legal collections of the Pentateuch, namely, the Covenant Code and the Deuteronomic Code.[34] In these two codes, the *gērim* are portrayed as *personae miserae* and are protected from

---

29. Milgrom, *Leviticus 17–22*, 1493–1501.

30. Ibid., 1496.

31. Ibid., 1497.

32. Ibid.

33. Ibid., 1499.

34. See Achenbach, "gêr," 30–32; or Albertz, "From Aliens," 54–56.

abuse. Milgrom himself also engages with these texts and the fact that these texts are there and that some of the *gērim* were vulnerable does not really detract from Milgrom's larger thesis.[35] The vulnerable *gērim* also had to obey the prohibitive commandments, even if they themselves had to be protected at times. The *second* text that does not fit simply into the explanation by Milgrom is Lev 19:33–34, where the addressees are asked to love the *gērim* as they love themselves. Earlier in verse 18 the addressees were asked to love their "neighbors" in a similar fashion. Some would simply regard this as another example of treating the *gēr* as a vulnerable person, and verse 33 supports this argument, but still it puts the *gēr* on the same level as the brother in verse 18.[36] Both should expect the love of the addressees.[37] Still, one should probably also add that in both cases the love commandment is used to achieve another goal. In verse 33, which also portrays the *gēr* as one of the *personae miserae*, the objective is not to oppress the *gēr*, whereas in verse 18 it was not to hold a grudge against your neighbor. When read with these goals in mind, it does not seem as if the neighbor and the stranger were regarded as exactly the same. The *gēr* leaves the impression of being much more vulnerable. A *third* problem also arises. If anybody—"Israelite or non-Israelite"—could pollute the land, as Milgrom put it in the first quote above, why then are *only* the *gērim* asked to obey certain rules? What about the *tôšābim*, for instance? Could they not also pollute the land? Why are they not included in many of the "prohibitive commandments"? I will return to most of these issues in the following discussion about the recent contributions of other scholars.

NIHAN

Recently Nihan has also presented an argument that the *gērim* in H are different from the portrayal of the *gērim* in the other legal codes, but also different from the *tôšāb* mentioned in H.[38] This is nothing new, but Nihan adds that the *gēr* is indeed economically independent whereas the *tôšāb* is economically dependent on the Israelites and is still regarded as "clients of

---

35. Milgrom, *Leviticus 17–22*, 1494.

36. See, for example, Joosten, *People and Land*, 59; or Albertz, "From Aliens," 57.

37. Milgrom, *Leviticus 17–22*, 1653 and 1706, is also adamant that "love" means something practical, both in verse 18 and verse 34. In both cases love can be a command, simply because it refers to deeds which are to be done to the neighbor and the stranger.

38. Nihan, "Resident Aliens," 118–24.

Israelite households."[39] Nihan still regards the *gērim* as legally inferior to the Israelites, despite the fact that they are economically independent.[40] For Nihan, the love commandment in Lev 19:34 is qualified by what follows afterwards, namely, a command not to cheat in business, which provides a resolution of the second problem above. The *gēr* should thus be treated like any other *'ezrāḥ*, especially when it comes to business.[41] Nihan mostly agrees with the interpretation by Milgrom, but argues that with regard to the legal status of the *gēr* there is one other important difference between the *'ezrāḥ* and the *gēr*. The *gēr* is not allowed to own land.[42] This is, according to him, especially clear in Leviticus 25, where there is no explicit indication that the *gērim* may own land. Thus even if a brother ends up in debt and needs to sell his land (or actually the remaining harvests to the next Jubilee), the *gēr* is never portrayed as the buyer of the land. The basic legal difference for Nihan between an Israelite and a *gēr* in H is that the latter may not own land.[43] One problem with this interpretation, however, has to do with the portrayal of the *gēr* in the last case in Leviticus 25. How did this *gēr* become rich? How could one be rich without land? In my understanding, the text acknowledges that in that historical reality the *gērim* did own land. There might still be a difference between the authors of H not regarding *gērim* as legal owners of land and the historical reality in the Persian period that *gērim* did own land. Thus if you focus exclusively on the text, Nihan might be right, but if you look at the historical context, *gērim* probably did own land.[44] Nihan also offers us a way out of the third problem identified above in the light of Milgrom's proposal. He describes the *gēr* as follows:[45]

---

39. Ibid., 119. Nihan acknowledges that Leviticus 19:9–10 and 23:22 are the only two examples where the *gēr* is portrayed similarly to the portrayals of *gērim* as dependent in the Covenant Code and Deuteronomic Code, as explained above when the first problem with Milgrom's proposal was presented.

40. Ibid., 121.

41. Ibid., 122.

42. Ibid., 123–24.

43. Rendtorff, "The *gēr*," 85, comes to a similar conclusion in the light of Ezek 47:22. He says that "the only thing that distinguishes a permanent *gēr* from an Israelite is the participation in the possession of land."

44. Nihan, "Resident Aliens," 131, thinks that the *gērim* might have included "wealthy merchant families, foreign soldiers, members for the Achaemenid administration, and so on." This seems like a realistic portrayal of life in Persian period Yehud, but still I find it difficult to imagine that these people never owned land.

45. Ibid., 130.

> Nonetheless, because the *gēr* resides in the land *alongside* the Israelites, and is considered in principle as a free person, he is also subject to a series of requirements at the level of H's *sacral* legislation. These requirements are united by the concern to prevent the possibility that the *gēr*, like the Israelite, may provoke the wrath of the patron deity either by profaning the sanctuary or by polluting the land. [Italics in original]

The *gērim* thus pose a threat *because* they are independent and free, and not like the *tôšābim*, for instance, who are dependent on an Israelite and therefore unfree.[46] In agreement with Milgrom, Nihan argues that the *gērim* were not really included in the cult. They are still allowed to practice profane slaughter, for instance (Lev 17:3–7).[47] For Nihan, H follows after the Deuteronomic Code (D) which means that everybody was allowed to practice profane slaughter in D, but now H modifies D by prohibiting Israelites from practicing profane slaughter. Yet the *gērim* may still do it, although verses 8 to 9 say that if the *gērim* want to bring an animal sacrifice to Yahweh, they must bring it to the sanctuary like the Israelites. Apart from the issue of the relationship between D and H, Nihan is mostly in agreement with Milgrom.

The most important difference pointed out by Nihan[48] which still draws clear boundaries between Israelites and *gērim*, as far as I am concerned, is the fact that "the *gēr* is consistently omitted from the exhortation to achieve holiness." This goes to the heart of the Holiness Code. The following texts are all from what is usually called the parenetic frame of the Holiness Code:[49]

> Speak to all the congregation of the people of Israel and say to them: You shall be holy, for I the Lord your God am holy (Lev 19:2 NRSV).

It is, of course, this kind of language which gives the name to the code and this is the first instance where people are commanded to be holy. The next two examples are from chapter 20. The motivation for their being holy is the fact that YHWH is holy.

---

46. In support, one could also refer to Lev 25:6. This text says that the harvest must be left for different groups to eat. The *gēr* is not mentioned as one of these groups, presuming that they are not dependent on the addressee and the others are.

47. For a similar argument, see Joosten, *People and Land*, 66.

48. Nihan, "Resident Aliens," 128–29.

49. See Otto, "Innerbiblische Exegese," 172–76.

7 Consecrate yourselves therefore, and be holy; for I am the Lord your God. 8 Keep my statutes, and observe them; I am the Lord; I sanctify you (Lev 20:7–8 NRSV).

It is clear that the Israelites are to be holy (whatever that might entail). Now YHWH is the one who makes them holy.

22 You shall keep all my statutes and all my ordinances, and observe them, so that the land to which I bring you to settle in may not vomit you out. 23 You shall not follow the practices of the nation that I am driving out before you. Because they did all these things, I abhorred them. 24 But I have said to you: You shall inherit their land, and I will give it to you to possess, a land flowing with milk and honey. I am the Lord your God; I have separated you from the peoples. 25 You shall therefore make a distinction between the clean animal and the unclean, and between the unclean bird and the clean; you shall not bring abomination on yourselves by animal or by bird or by anything with which the ground teems, which I have set apart for you to hold unclean. 26 You shall be holy to me; for I the Lord am holy, and I have separated you from the other peoples to be mine (Lev 20:22–26 NRSV).

From this text, it is clear that holiness overlaps with being separated from other nations. Verse 25 takes us back to Leviticus 11 in the first half of Leviticus. Mixed into this text one also finds themes such as the gift of land as well as the threat that the land might vomit out the addressees, as it did with earlier inhabitants. Although, as Nihan points out, "it is nowhere stated in H that achievement of holiness is not possible for the resident alien," the *gēr* is never included in this quest for holiness.[50] The quest is reserved for Israel. This is one of the main differences between Israel and the *gērim*. The authors of H believed that the Israelites were capable of becoming holy like YHWH is holy, but it seems that they did not include the *gērim* in this rather positive view.

ETHICS AND HOLINESS

If one were to attempt to engage with the ethics of the Holiness Code, these exhortations to be holy might be a good place to start, especially a text such as Lev 19:2. It is expected of the addressees to be holy and as motivation the holiness of YHWH is mentioned. For Milgrom, there is an element

50. Nihan, "Resident Aliens," 128.

of *imitatio dei* in this text. Milgrom is careful to argue that Lev 19:2 does not mean that Israel can "imitate YHWH's holiness."[51] For Milgrom, there is an "unbridgeable gap" between the holiness of YHWH and the kind of holiness Israel can aspire to. He even points out that the adjective for holy is spelled differently when applied to humans and to YHWH.[52] When discussing Leviticus 19, Milgrom distinguishes between negative and positive commands and then argues:

> In this latter [positive commands] sense, holiness implies *imitatio dei*, namely, Israel should emulate God by living a godly life. Observance of the divine commandments leads to God's attribute of holiness, but not to the same degree—not to God, but to godliness.[53]

Israel is thus to imitate certain acts of YHWH, but cannot really be like God. The acts Israel need to imitate include acts like caring for the poor and vulnerable people in society, loving the neighbor and the *gēr*, and obeying the other commandments.

In 1999, Edwin Firmage wrote a fascinating article entitled "Genesis 1 and the Priestly Agenda."[54] Whereas many scholars have traditionally attributed Lev 11:43–45 to H, Firmage argues that the whole of chapter 11 belongs to H.[55] Leviticus 11 is, of course, the chapter that prescribes what should be eaten and what not, and towards the end of the chapter one finds the following verses:

> 43 You shall not make yourselves detestable with any creature that swarms; you shall not defile yourselves with them, and so become unclean. 44 For I am the Lord your God; sanctify yourselves therefore, and be holy, for I am holy. You shall not defile yourselves with

---

51. Milgrom, *Leviticus 17–22*, 1397–1400.

52. Ibid., 1398. In Lev 11:44, 45; 19:2; 20:7 (see text critical note in BHS), 26 and 21:8, where the adjective refers to YHWH, the *plene* form (*qādôš*) is used. When the adjective is applied to human beings (Lev 11:44, 45; 19:2; 20:7, 26; 21:6, 7), the defective form (*qādōš*) is used.

53. Ibid., 1398.

54. Firmage, "Genesis 1," 97–114.

55. Ibid., 113. He believes that chapter 11 is a "dislocated H fragment." See the critical discussion by Nihan, *Priestly Torah*, 299 notes 139 and 303, who shows that older scholars such as Driver and Horst have already presented this view. The main problem with Driver and Horst and now also with Firmage is as Nihan, *Priestly Torah*, 303, puts it, is "that H's terminology and characteristic motifs are limited to 11:43–45 and are simply missing from the remainder of the chapter." The same criticism goes for Genesis 1.

any swarming creature that moves on the earth. 45 For I am the
Lord who brought you up from the land of Egypt, to be your God;
you shall be holy, for I am holy (Lev 11:43–45 NRSV).

For Firmage, the right eating advocated by H fits best into the ideal
of holiness for ordinary people.[56] But Firmage makes another link which is
even more radical.[57] He also believes that Genesis 1 is part of H. For him,
there is a clear link between humanity made in the image of God in Genesis
1:27 and the expectation of the Holiness Code that Israel should follow
in God's footsteps and be as holy as him. Even if one does not accept his
arguments that Genesis 1 is part of H, one could still argue that although
H is later than P (which includes Genesis 1), H shares the positive view of
the ability of Israel to be like God with its Priestly predecessors, i.e., *if* there
is a link between becoming holy and being made in the image of God (an
issue we will return to in a moment). For Firmage, the holiness ideal of H
would not have been possible without the idea of Genesis 1 that humanity
was created in the image of God. The Holiness Code thus has a very positive anthropology. Israel could become holy like God and this was because
humanity was created in the image of God in the first place.

But the problem remains for our discussion, as Nihan pointed out,
that the *gēr* is not included in the ideal that Israel should be holy. Even if
the authors of Genesis 1, which we can regard as part of P, originally had
a positive view of all of humanity, the same cannot be said of their priestly
descendants in H. For the authors of H, only Israelites could be holy and
they did not include the *gērim*. They (the *gērim*) are included in laws which
will keep them from polluting the land and Israel, but the positive ideal of
Israel becoming holy like YHWH is never applied to them. The important
question is whether the authors of H never thought that the strangers were
also included in Gen 1:27. Or should we take a step back and ask whether
there really is a link between being made between the image of God and
being holy, as Firmage makes suggests? Is there any other evidence that H
was closely acquainted with the creation theology of P? Are there any other
explicit theological links made between H and the first creation narrative?

Good arguments have been put forward for at least two important
theological links. These have to do with the Sabbath and the use of the
Hebrew root *bdl* (divide, separate etc.). The Sabbath is central to H, especially as found in Leviticus 23, 25, and 26—an argument forcefully made by

56. Firmage, "Genesis 1," 107–8.

57. Ibid., 110–11.

Andreas Ruwe.[58] The authors of H were thus clearly building on Gen 2:1–4a. They also share the same concern about order and the fairly rare verbal root *bdl* is found in texts such as Leviticus 20 and Genesis 1. Just as YHWH distinguished between day and night, for instance, the authors of Leviticus 20 called on Israel to distinguish (*bdl*) between clean and unclean (v. 25) and (*bdl*) to be separated from the nations around them by YHWH (vv. 24 and 26). Thus, one could argue with regard to the Sabbath and a worldview dominated by the notion of order[59] that H was indeed well acquainted with the theology of P.

Yet, is there really a link (as Firmage would have it) between "made in the image of God" in Genesis 1 and the exhortation to be holy in the Holiness Code? As far as I can see, there is not.[60] None of the important concepts in Gen 1:26–27 with regard to humanity being made in the image of God is ever repeated in the Holiness Code. Furthermore, if there is some link between "made in the image of God" and being holy, why did the authors not spell it out, as they did with the Sabbath? The text never says "be holy, because you were made in my image"! In Lev 11:46 and 19:2, the motivation for the command to be holy is supplied (in the former only) by means of a reference to Egypt and (in both) a reference to the holiness of YHWH. In Lev 19:34, when the addressees are asked to love the *gēr* as themselves, the same motivation of deliverance from Egypt is used, but there is never any mention of being created in the image of God. One could argue that if one read the rest of P in Genesis, and especially the flood narrative, that the authors of P did not really think much was left of this image of God in humanity. The image of God in humanity was probably spoiled by the violence and total corruption of which we read in Gen 6:11–12 in the P part of the flood narrative. Theologically, liberation from Egypt is important, but *imago dei* is never used as a theological motivation. It thus seems clear that there is no link between the quest for holiness and the concept

58. See Ruwe, "*Heiligkeitzgesetz*," 90–97. Ruwe's argument focuses more on Leviticus 23 and 25 and the fact that he did not engage with chapter 26 (apart from the first two verses) could be regarded as one of the weaknesses of his book. Leviticus 26 clearly builds on the Sabbath with the noun occurring five times (vv. 2, 34 [x2], 35, and 43) and the verb four times (vv. 6, 34, and 35 [x2]). Still, for Ruwe, the "Sabbatthematik" is the main theme of the second part of the Holiness Code.

59. See discussion in Meyer, "Divide," 1–6.

60. I am indebted to Prof. Dr. Thomas Hieke of Johannes Gutenberg University in Mainz for the main argument in this paragraph. I am drawing from an email discussion we had during September and October 2013 on this topic. I look forward to his commentary on Leviticus in the Herder series.

of *imago dei,* and consequently that Firmage is wrong in this regard. But where does this leave us with the *gērim*? What could we possibly learn from the way in which the *gērim* are portrayed in Leviticus?

CONCLUSION

It should be clear by now that the *gērim* in Leviticus 16–26 were not proselytes. Apart from Milgrom and Nihan, other scholars such as Joosten,[61] Ramírez Kidd,[62] and Zehnder[63] have reached similar conclusions. Including the *gērim* in some obligations does not constitute an act of incorporating them into Israel; it is in essence an act of protecting Israel from losing its land. The *gērim* are never understood as being the same as the Israelites, even if it becomes clear that they are economically independent, as Nihan pointed out. Nihan also made it clear that the *gērim* were not included in the quest for holiness, which also accentuates their difference. We also saw that there are no links within the texts between the quest for holiness and the *imago dei* of Genesis 1. Yet one should also acknowledge that, at times, the *gērim* were protected by the laws of the Holiness Code.

One could argue rather cynically that the fact that the *gērim* were seen as a threat to the relationship Israel had with YHWH and the land is an expression of xenophobia. Indeed, one does find the fear that the *gērim* might bedevil things, yet this fear is not reserved for the *gērim*, but also applied to the Israelites. Most of these laws are addressed to the Israelite addressees and they themselves posed the greatest threat to their own survival on the land. It is not as if the *gērim* would be *more* inclined to mess things up than the addressees, simply because they are strangers! The texts never give that impression and an argument for xenophobia can thus (thankfully) not be made.

What is striking about the *gērim* in Leviticus, though, is that there never seems to be any attempt to get rid of them. Ramírez Kidd sums up the attitude of the authors toward the *gēr* in the Holiness Code as follows:

> Their approach is pragmatic, it answers the question: *what should be done if a gēr living in Israel wants . . .* to offer an offering, to celebrate Passover or if he blasphemes Yahweh's name? The Holiness Code and P simply acknowledge the presence of the *gēr* among the

61. Joosten, *People and Land,* 71–72.

62. Ramírez Kidd, *Alterity,* 64–67.

63. Zehnder, *Umgang mit Fremden,* 349.

people, and attempt to define the rules which provide the preservation of holiness in the land. [Italics in original][64]

It seems that the authors of H have made peace with the presence of the *gērim* in their midst and the question was a pragmatic one. It is also striking that the *gērim* are given a fair amount of freedom. Joosten puts it as follows:[65]

> As a resident alien, he is a free agent and nobody's charge. The law therefore seeks to protect him from oppression and recommends him to the goodwill of the Israelites. His freedom is real: the *gēr* may retain his foreign culture and religion[66] with its practices, though he would be welcome to participate in the Israelite religion with its practices. In any case, however, he should observe the apodictic prohibitions for fear of defiling the land and the sanctuary, the earthly dwelling of YHWH among the people.

There is thus no expectation of the *gēr* to become Israelite, but he/she has certain privileges and certain limited obligations. The fact that the *gērim* were not proselytes actually becomes something good. Proselyting could become a very hegemonic force when it becomes a prerequisite for staying in the land. There is nothing of that in these texts. When one reads of concepts such as "pragmatism" (Ramírez Kidd) and "freedom" (Joosten), one wonders what role the broader Persian Empire played in this view of the *gērim*. These abstract nouns are sometimes used to describe Persian rule in this period, especially when it comes to the religious freedom the Persians gave their subjects.[67]

It should be obvious that we are also in need of this kind of pragmatism and freedom in our world. Pragmatism helps us to make peace with the world as it is, but also to find a way to cope with what we have, a way which is just and fair. Freedom is something we need to give to others who are different from "us." "They" need the freedom to be different from us,

---

64. Ramírez Kidd, *Alterity*, 69.

65. Joosten, *People and Land*, 72.

66. Ibid., 65–69, makes a strong case that in the light of texts such as Lev 17:3 and 24:15 the *gērim* were allowed to worship their own gods. See also Nihan, "Resident Aliens," 115.

67. See overview provided by Gerstenberger, *Israel in der Perserzeit*, 54–55. Or, see a much more critical overview by Balentine, *Torah's Vision*, 42–57. Yes, the Persians gave their subjects religious freedom and limited autonomy and even paid for the rebuilding of the temple, but these acts can all be understood as "Mechanisms of Social Control."

while at the same time receiving respect and protection from us. Apparently, these concepts were well understood by the authors of H.

BIBLIOGRAPHY

Achenbach, Reinhard. "gêr—nåkhrî—tôshav—zâr: Legal and Sacral Distinctions regarding Foreigners in the Pentateuch." In *The Foreigner and the Law: Perspectives from the Hebrew Bible and the Ancient Near East*, edited by Reinhard Achenbach, Rainer Albertz, and Jakob Wöhrle, 29–51. Beihefte zur Zeitschrift für altorientalische und biblische Rechtsgeschichte 16. Wiesbaden: Harrassowitz, 2011.

Albertz, Rainer. "From Aliens to Proselytes: Non-Priestly and Priestly Legislation Concerning Strangers." In *The Foreigner and the Law: Perspectives from the Hebrew Bible and the Ancient Near East*, edited by Reinhard Achenbach, Rainer Albertz, and Jakob Wöhrle, 53–69. Beihefte zur Zeitschrift für altorientalische und biblische Rechtsgeschichte. Wiesbaden: Harrassowitz, 2011.

Balentine, Samuel E. *The Torah's Vision of Worship*. Overtures to Biblical Theology. Minneapolis, MN: Fortress, 1999.

Cholewinski, Alfred. *Heiligkeitsgesetz und Deuteronomium: Eine vergleichende Studie*. Analecta Biblica 66. Rome: Biblical Institute Press, 1976.

Elliger, Karl. *Leviticus*. Handbuch zum Alten Testament I/4. Tübingen: Mohr, 1966.

Firmage, Edwin. "Genesis 1 and the Priestly Agenda." *JSOT* 82 (1999) 97–114.

Gerstenberger, Erhard S. *Das 3. Buch Mose. Leviticus*. Das Alte Testament Deutsch 6. Göttingen: VandenHoeck & Ruprecht, 1993.

———. *Israel in der Perserzeit. 5. und 4. Jahrhundert v. Chr*. Biblische Enzyklopädie 8. Stuttgart: Kohlhammer, 2005.

Joosten, Jan. *People and Land in the Holiness Code: An Exegetical Study of the Ideational Framework of the Law in Leviticus 17–26*. Supplement to Vetus Testamentum 67. Leiden: Brill, 1996.

Knohl, Israel. *The Sanctuary of Silence: The Priestly Torah and the Holiness School*. Minneapolis, MN: Fortress, 1995.

Meyer, Esias E. "Divide and be Different: Priestly Identity in the Persian period." *HTS Teologiese Studies/Theological Studies* 68/1 (2012) 1–6.

———. *The Jubilee in Leviticus 25: A Theological Ethical Interpretation from a South African Perspective*. Exegese in unserer Zeit 15. Münster, Lit Verlag, 2005.

Milgrom, Jacob. *Leviticus 1–16: A New Translation with Introduction and Commentary*. The Anchor Yale Bible 3. New Haven, CT: Yale University Press, 1991.

———. *Leviticus 17–22: A New Translation with Introduction and Commentary*. The Anchor Yale Bible 3A. New Haven, CT: Yale University Press, 2000.

Nihan, Christophe. *From Priestly Torah to Pentateuch: A Study in the Composition of the Book of Leviticus*. Forschungen zum Alten Testament II/25. Tübingen: Mohr Siebeck, 2007.

——— "Resident Aliens and Natives in the Holiness Legislation." In *The Foreigner and the Law: Perspectives from the Hebrew Bible and the Ancient Near East*, edited by Reinhard Achenbach, Rainer Albertz, and Jakob Wöhrle, 111–33. Beihefte zur Zeitschrift für altorientalische und biblische Rechtsgeschichte 16. Wiesbaden: Harrassowitz, 2011.

Otto, Eckart. "Innerbiblische Exegese im Heiligkeitsgesetz Levitikus 17–26." In *Levitikus als Buch*, edited by Heinz-Josef Fabry and Hans-Winfried Jüngling, 125–96. Bonner Biblische Beiträge 119. Bonn: Philo, 1999.

Ramírez Kidd, José E. *Alterity and Identity in Israel: The גר in the Old Testament.* Beihefte zur Zeitschrift für die alttestamentliche Wissenschaft 283. Berlin: de Gruyter 1999.

Rendtorff, Rolf. "The *gēr* in the Priestly Laws of the Pentateuch." In *Ethnicity and the Bible*, edited by Mark G. Brett, 77–87. Biblical Interpretation Series 19. Leiden: Brill, 2002.

Ruwe, Andreas. *"Heiligkeitzgesetz" und "Priesterschrift." Literaturgeschichtliche und rechtssystematische Untersuchungen zu Leviticus 17,1—26,2.* Forschungen zum Alten Testament 26. Tübingen: Mohr Siebeck, 1999.

Sparks, Kenton L. *Ethnicity and Identity in Ancient Israel: Prolegomena to the Study of Ethnic Sentiments and Their Expression in the Hebrew Bible.* Winona Lake, IN: Eisenbrauns, 1998.

Van Houten, Christiana. *The Alien in Israelite Law.* Journal for the Study of the Old Testament Supplement 107. Sheffield, UK: Sheffield Academic Press, 1991.

Zehnder, Markus. *Umgang mit Fremden in Israel und Assyrien. Ein Beitrag zur Anthropologie des "Fremden" im Licht antiker Quellen.* Beiträge zur Wissenschaft vom Alten und Neuen Testament 168. Stuttgart: Kohlhammer, 2005.

7

De-Ideologizing Ezra-Nehemiah:
Challenging Discriminatory Ideologies

Ntozakhe Cezula,
Faculty of Theology, Stellenbosch University

INTRODUCTION

SINCE THE 1990S THERE has increasingly been a call for a theology of reconstruction in Africa and particularly for a biblical paradigm for such a theology, similar to the exodus/Moses biblical paradigm which was prominent during the liberation struggles of the previously colonized countries.[1] According to Jesse Mugambi, Nehemiah is one such possible biblical paradigm for a theology of reconstruction in Africa. One should note, however, that Ezra-Nehemiah has in the past been read by activists of discriminatory ideologies, such as the Nazis in Germany and proponents of apartheid in South Africa, to justify their actions. And it may well be that there will be such readers in the future again. In this regard, Elelwani Farisani argues that for a theology of renewal, reform, transformation, reconciliation, and

---

1. Mugambi, *Christian Theology*, 172–73.

reconstruction to be effective, it will have to be conscious that the Ezra-Nehemiah text is not neutral. Farisani consistently argues that a theology of reconstruction will have to take seriously, "in its theological backing of the process of renewal and transformation in Africa, the fact that each and every text in the Bible is the product of its socio-historical context."[2] He furthermore suggests that, in order to avoid the oppression and silencing of the already marginalized poor, the text's ideology has to be subjected to a rigorous sociological analysis so as to de-ideologize it.

In this essay, I will seek to re-read Ezra-Nehemiah in order to contribute to the discourse on reconstruction theology in (South) Africa.[3] In order, however, to classify as a restorative reading, I propose that it is vitally important to de-ideologize the text. For this purpose, it will be important to consider relevant aspects of the socio-historical context of Ezra-Nehemiah in addition to identifying competing ideologies in Ezra-Nehemiah and its contemporaries. Some of the reconstruction projects taking place in Ezra-Nehemiah and Chronicles will also be examined, together with the identity processes informing them to assess their ideological effects. In the first section, however, some introductory remarks regarding the relevance of Ezra-Nehemiah for reconstruction in Africa will be introduced.

RELEVANCE OF EZRA–NEHEMIAH IN AN AFRICAN CONTEXT

According to Nupanga Weanzana, Ezra-Nehemiah is "the source for what African theologians have for some years been calling the theology of reconstruction."[4] He argues that this approach sees the present situation of the African continent as comparable in varying degrees to that of the Jewish community on their return from exile. In highlighting the African situation, Weanzana argues as follows:

> Although various countries regained their independence in the 1960s, the African continent has not been able to achieve political,

2. Farisani, *Ezra-Nehemiah*, 297.

3. While Africa is a greatly diverse continent with different political and social situations, it is also true that ethnic conflict has been one of the widespread social ills that have hindered progress in reconstructing this continent since decolonization. For this reason, this article is concerned with the African situation in general but expressing it through the particular situation of South Africa, hence the expression (South) Africa.

4. Weanzana, "Ezra," 532.

social or religious cohesion. It is still influenced and fascinated by foreign nations that are regarded both as models to be emulated and scapegoats to blame for all problems. Consequently, this continent needs reconstruction in the spiritual, social and economic spheres. The books of Ezra and Nehemiah contain some guidelines on how to achieve this.[5]

However, unlike Weanzana, who seeks to identify aspects from Ezra-Nehemiah to emulate, I will focus on what to avoid from Ezra-Nehemiah. This approach becomes even more crucial when taking note of what Weanzana highlights, namely, that Ezra and Nehemiah also present the interaction of divine and human activity in the process of reconstruction.[6] While Weanzana rightfully perceives this interaction in the light of God using humans as instruments for God's mission, one also sees evidence of the author's/authors' perception of their own context that plays an important role in changing perceptions and forming opinions. Gale Yee says it well:

> The Bible was not written to be an object of aesthetic beauty or contemplation, but as a persuasive force forming opinion, making judgments, and exerting change. It was a form of power acting upon the world.[7]

This sentiment finds expression, for example, in what Louis Jonker calls *rhetorical studies* of Chronicles, with the central question of: "What did the book Chronicles want to achieve?" Jonker writes:

> The peculiar literary formation of this book was now interpreted as an indication that Chronicles was an attempt to bolster certain ideological and/or theological positions (e.g., the position of the Levites in the Second Temple cultic community). The presentation of figures of the past in Chronicles was no longer seen as a reflection of past realities, but rather as idealization serving particular rhetorical purposes in a new present (the time of origin of Chronicles).[8]

In view of this approach, I propose that it is important to de-ideologize Ezra-Nehemiah if the book is to be read with the intention of participating in the quest for a theology of reconstruction in Africa. By de-ideologization,

---

5. Ibid., 532.
6. Ibid.
7. Yee, "The Author," 116.
8. Jonker, *1 & 2 Chronicles*, 4.

I do not mean to strip the text of its ideology and thereby render it ideol-
ogy-free. For me, that is somewhat idealistic. Narratives are ideological,
and ideologies are manifest in narratives. Instead, by de-ideologization I
refer basically to two processes. The first is to identify the ideology in the
text; i.e., to raise awareness regarding the dominant ideology. The second
is to bring forward other ideologies that compete with the dominant ideology, with the purpose of allowing the readers of Ezra-Nehemiah to choose
an ideology that promises to serve reconstruction in Africa best. In other
words, de-ideologization, as utilized in this essay, helps the reader to see beyond what is presented to them, thereby freeing them from the confines of
the dominant ideology and providing them with the freedom to choose.[9] In
this essay, I will seek to de-ideologize Ezra-Nehemiah by first showing that
there is an exclusivist ethnic ideology in Ezra-Nehemiah. Thereafter, I will
bring forward other ideologies that competed with the dominant ideology
in Ezra-Nehemiah during the Second Temple period in Judah. By doing
this, I hope to create a wider pool of Second Temple ideologies in Judah to
choose from in the quest for a theology of reconstruction in Africa. Before
any further attempt to de-ideologize Ezra-Nehemiah, however, the discussion must look at some previous readings of Ezra-Nehemiah that reinforce
this idea of the de-ideologization of this book.

SOME PREVIOUS READINGS OF EZRA-NEHEMIAH

Ezra 9 and 10 are two quite dramatic chapters in Ezra, outlining a crisis regarding the marriages between Judean leaders and women from the people
of the land (Ezra 9:2). Ezra views these marriages first as the breaking of the
Law, and secondly, as the same sin that led to the exile (Ezra 9:6–15). The
crisis is resolved by separating the Judahites from their foreign wives (Ezra
10:1–44). All this drama is rooted in the belief that mixing with foreigners
is disobedience to God (Ezra 9:10–12).

---

9. An example of this approach is found in Elelwani Farisani's thesis, titled "The
Use of Ezra-Nehemiah in a Quest for a Theology of Renewal, Transformation and Reconstruction in the (South) African Context." What Farisani does in this study is first to
demonstrate that Ezra-Nehemiah contains a particular exclusivist ideology which tends
to be biased against the עַם הָאָרֶץ, while being biased in favor of the returned exiles.
Secondly, Farisani attempts to retrieve the voices of the marginalized עַם הָאָרֶץ and then
proceeds to read Ezra-Nehemiah from the perspective of the עַם הָאָרֶץ. By so doing, he
hopes to sensitize theologians to the voices and needs of all stakeholders in the renewal
and transformation of Africa.

This discriminatory behavior on the part of Ezra-Nehemiah has been employed by some readers who subscribed to discriminatory ideologies for justification of their actions. For instance, at the Nuremberg trial proceedings on Friday, April 26, 1946, the Nazi activist, Julius Streicher, who had been publisher, editor, and a writer for the German newspaper *Der Stürmer*, was accused of crimes against humanity. He was then asked whether he was consulted about the planning and preparation of the draft of the Nuremberg Laws of 1935 and whether he had any part in their preparation. These laws were believed to have been responsible for the elimination of Jews from Germany which later resulted in the Holocaust. In his answer, Streicher said:

> Yes, I believe I had a part in it insofar as for years I have written that any further mixture of German blood with Jewish blood must be avoided. I have written such articles again and again; and in my articles I have repeatedly emphasized the fact that the Jews should serve as an example to every race, for they created a racial law for themselves—the Law of Moses, which says, "If you come into a foreign land you shall not take unto yourself foreign women." And that, Gentlemen, is of tremendous importance in judging the Nuremberg Laws. These laws of the Jews were taken as a model for these laws. When, after centuries, the Jewish lawgiver Ezra discovered that notwithstanding many Jews had married non-Jewish women, these marriages were dissolved. That was the beginning of Jewry which, because it introduced these racial laws, has survived throughout the centuries, while all other races and civilizations have perished.[10]

The text to which Streicher is referring here is Ezra 9–10 which he uses in order to justify his participation in the Nuremberg laws. Closer to home, the apartheid system in South Africa was also based on a particular understanding of the importance of separation between people as reflected in the book Ezra-Nehemiah. Motivating his assertion that God's blessing rests upon apartheid, one professor of New Testament exegesis and theology at the University of Pretoria, Prof. Dr. E. P. Groenewald, argued as follows:

> This truth is confirmed in the history of Christianity. The Lord who willed the segregation of the nations, abundantly blessed the

10. *Nuremberg Trial Proceedings*, 315.

nations which respected His stipulation and also used them as a blessing to humanity in general.[11]

It is interesting to note that Groenewald also considered Nehemiah to be a helpful analogy. Arguing for what he calls *social apartheid*, in addition to *national apartheid* and *religious apartheid*, he states:

> To Israel the Lord instructs that there should be no mixing with foreign nations.[12] . . . The Scripture views it generally as a deviation from the will of God when Israel allows that her sons and daughters marry with other nations. Such marriages let national differences grow faint and lead to undermining of the mother tongue. The result is a generation that does not honor or even know its own language, customs, religion and also nationality. So writes Nehemiah (13:23).[13]

Groenewald perceives Neh 13:23 as a good and a reliable source for his separatist argument. Furthermore, in March 1947 a report of a ministers' conference near Pretoria at which 150 delegates discussed a United Nations resolution on South Africa appeared in *Op Die Horison* in which a distinction between the *direct* and *indirect* scriptural evidence for apartheid was made. Texts like Ezra 9:3, 10: 2, 9, 10, 14, 17, and Neh 13:23–25, among others, were identified as *indirect* biblical proofs in addition to *direct* biblical proofs such as Gen 10: 5, 20, 31, Deut 32:8, and selected New Testament verses such as Acts 17:26, Rev 5:9, etc.[14]

The point being made here is that the book of Ezra-Nehemiah has been read in the past to justify ideologies that were later declared to be gross violations of human rights. The concern of this essay is that in the

11. This is my own translation from Afrikaans. In Afrikaans it is stated as follows: "Hierdie waarheid is in die geskiedenis van die Christendom bevestig. Die Here wat die apartheid van die volke gewil het, het ook die volke wat Sy bepaling geëerbiedig het, ryklik geseën en tot seën vir die mensheid in die algemeen gebruik," Groenewald, "Apartheid," 52.

12. A quotation from Deut 7:2–4.

13. In this regard, Groenewald quotes Neh 13:23. Also, this is my own translation from Afrikaans which says: "Aan Israel beveel die Here dat daar geen vermenging met vreemde nasies mag wees nie. . . . Die Skrif beskou dit deurgaans as 'n afwyking van die wil van God wanneer Israel toelaat dat sy seuns en dogters met dié van ander volke trou. Sulke huwelike laat die nasionale skeidinge vervaag en gee aanleiding tot 'n geringskatting van die moedertaal. Die resultaat is 'n geslag wat hul eie taal, sedes, godsdiens en ook nasionaliteit nie meer eerbiedig of selfs ken nie. So skryf Nehemia (13: 23)," Groenewald, "Apartheid," 52–53.

14. Loubser, *Apartheid Bible*, 58.

future there may once again be readers who might hold discriminatory ideologies and use Ezra-Nehemiah as a justification for such ideologies. This essay proposes that, while Ezra-Nehemiah has been said to be relevant for reconstruction in Africa, such reading of Ezra-Nehemiah cannot serve the best interests of reconstruction in Africa. For the Ezra-Nehemiah narrative to contribute positively to the reconstruction of Africa, we need a reading of this corpus that will protect the interests of *all* who live in Africa. It is against this background that this article supports the de-ideologization of Ezra-Nehemiah. In order for de-ideologization to be effectively implemented, the text needs to be put in its socio-historical context, which will be the topic of the next section.

SOME SOCIO-HISTORICAL ASPECTS OF EZRA-NEHEMIAH

My view is that when dealing with Second Temple literature, it is essential to take the exilic period into consideration. This places one in a better vantage point to understand the socio-historical context of the Second Temple period, because the Babylonian exile is a watershed period in the history of Israel. According to Daniel Smith-Christopher:

> The exile continued to have serious implications both internally as well as externally, long after the fall of the Neo-Babylonian Empire. Internally, the separation of the community in 597–586 began to create long-standing divisions (Ezek. 11:14–18, 33:23–27) that persisted after groups of diaspora Jews returned to Palestine under Persian patronage (thus Ezra 3–6 and the conflicts detailed there), particularly when one notes Ezra the priest using sectarian terminology ("sons of Exile") to refer to those with diaspora lineage as the true community in Palestine (Ezra 9).[15]

The events in Ezra-Nehemiah also need to be understood in this light, i.e., as the climax of a progressive tension which originated from the internal divisions created by the separation of the Judean community in 597–586 BC. Echoing a similar understanding, Carolyn Sharp notices divergent Jeremianic voices in the book of Jeremiah. According to Sharp, this can be seen to reflect political tensions of significant proportions between a stream of Deutero-Jeremianic tradition concerned to underwrite the authority of the Judeans exiled to Babylon in 597 and a Judah-based stream

15. Smith-Christopher, "Exile," 440.

of Deutero-Jeremianic tradition focused only on the inevitable doom threatening Judah and Jerusalem.[16] In the prophetic books of Jeremiah and Ezekiel there is thus evidence of a division between exiles and remainees. In Jer 24:10 and in Ezek 11:14–18 and 33:23–27, it is explicit that, during the exile, tension developed between the Judeans who were in exile and those who remained behind. Paul Hanson takes this division to another level when he argues that such polemical confrontations between the conflicting claims of the exilic community and the inhabitants of Jerusalem before the return of the exiles to Palestine made even more acrimonious confrontation inevitable once the return had taken place. Referring to Ezra, Hanson states that the returnees, carrying with them a program of restoration which was bound to an exclusive claim to being Yahweh's chosen community, refused to permit "the people of the land" to cooperate with them in the rebuilding efforts.[17]

Hanson is specific about these antagonistic groups in postexilic Yehud. He describes the rulers as "a very exclusive, and even intolerant, Zadokite-led hierocratic group . . . legitimized by the prestigious name of Ezekiel and authorized by the official decree of the Persian Emperor."[18] The other group he describes as the alienated and disenfranchised groups mainly comprised of the Trito-Isaiah prophetic group and their allies—the alienated Levites.[19] In brief, the writing of Ezra-Nehemiah took place within a context of an internal conflict between the Judeans: exiles versus remainees. Thus, in writing the narrative of Ezra-Nehemiah, the author(s) responded to these internal divisions that were prevalent at the time. It is with this context in mind that the discussion now moves to the task of de-ideologizing the text.

THE DE–IDEOLOGIZATION OF EZRA–NEHEMIAH

The task of de-ideologizing Ezra-Nehemiah is twofold: First, to distinguish the ideology underlying the text, and second, to bring to the fore other ideologies that compete with the dominant ideology in Ezra-Nehemiah. In the previous section, it has been established that Ezra-Nehemiah was written in the context of an internal conflict among the Second Temple Judeans. Central to this conflict is an identity crisis of being either an Israelite

16. Sharp, *Prophecy and Ideology in Jeremiah*, xiii.

17. Hanson, *The Dawn of Apocalyptic*, 242.

18. Ibid., 227; cf. also Ezra 4:3.

19. Ibid., 226–27.

or a foreigner. In an attempt to distinguish Ezra-Nehemiah's ideology, the concept of "foreigners" (בְּנֵי נֵכָר/נָכְרִי) will be scrutinized in order to uncover its role in the ideological strategies of Ezra-Nehemiah. This will be done by examining three expressions in the text: "the people of the land" (עַם הָאָרֶץ), "all Israel" (כָל-יִשְׂרָאֵל), and the "enemies" (אִיבִים/צָרִים). Other ideologies that competed with Ezra-Nehemiah's ideology will also be identified, particularly the ideology found in the book of Chronicles.

"People of the Land" (עַם הָאָרֶץ)

A close reading of Ezra-Nehemiah reveals that the concept "foreigners" includes elements that were not included in the previous understandings of these concepts. The reference to "the foreigners" is found beyond the traditional reference to non-Israelite national groups. One of the expressions that has been affected by this change is the reference to the "people of the land" (עַם הָאָרֶץ). According to Lynn Tatum, when this expression is used in reference to the pre-monarchic era, it simply signifies the free citizens of the particular locale under discussion;[20] in this sense, the term appears to exclude slaves and foreigners.[21] In the postexilic era, "the term takes on a negative aura. . . . It is now the returnees, those purified by the Exile, which represent the true congregation in contradistinction to all the "peoples of the land(s)."[22]

Some scholars argue that the "foreigners" in Ezra-Nehemiah are in fact Judeans who remained behind when others were taken as captives. Lester Grabbe is one of the scholars who argue along these lines. His argument is as follow:

> The conclusion seems straightforward: the text simply refuses to admit that there were Jewish inhabitants of the land after the deportations under Nebuchadnezzar. Probably only a minority of the people were taken away, with the tens of thousands still left. . . . There is no suggestion that any foreign peoples were brought in to replace those deported. . . . Instead we find references to the "peoples of the land" who are identified as foreigners. One can only conclude that many, if not all, of these "peoples of the land"

20. "Now Joseph was governor over the land; it was he who sold to all the people of the land" (Gen 42:6).

21. Tatum, "People of the Land," 1027.

22. Ibid.

were the Jewish descendants of those who were not deported. In the eyes of the author of Ezra, these peoples were no longer kin; the only "people of Israel" were those who had gone into captivity.[23]

Moreover, Elelwani Farisani is of the same opinion as Grabbe when he argues that "[t]he words 'our adversaries' or 'our enemies' צָרֵינוּ and 'people of the land' עַם הָאָרֶץ, 'peoples of the lands' עַמֵּי הָאֲרָצוֹת, refer to the people of the land, namely the Israelites who did not go to Babylonian exile, but remained in Palestine. Throughout the text the 'adversaries' צָרֵינוּ are introduced as opposing the returned exiles."[24]

I propose that in the case of Ezra-Nehemiah, the designation "foreigner" has become an ideological expression. It transformed an inclusive designation to exclude even *bona fide* Israelites, so becoming a tool for an exclusivist ethnic ideology.

"All Israel" (כָּל־יִשְׂרָאֵל)

The concept of "all Israel" appears eight times in the book of Ezra-Nehemiah. The idea is expressed in other forms as well, but the exact expression occurs eight times.[25] On one occasion, the concept is used referring to the monarchic period (Neh 13:26). It refers to King Solomon and his subjects as "all Israel." In other words, this term refers to the twelve tribes as they were before the schism. In five instances, "all Israel" is used to describe the exiles under the leadership of Ezra and Nehemiah (Ezra 2:70; 8:25; 10:5; Neh 2:73 [MT 2:72]; 12:47), specifically referring to the Babylonian exiles. Two times, this term is used specifically with reference to the twelve tribes as represented in the Second Temple exilic community (Ezra 6:17; 8:35).

Nehemiah 13:26 moreover employs the concept "all Israel" as a reference to a confederation of twelve Israelite tribes. Texts like Ezra 2:70, 8:25, 10:5, and Neh 2:73 [MT 2:72]; 12:47, however, have a different scenario in mind when referring to "all Israel." In these verses, Israel, which used to comprise twelve tribes, is reduced to Judah and Benjamin as those who were in exile. "All Israel" in these verses therefore suggests that when all Judahite and Benjaminite exiles are gathered together, the whole nation of Israel is present; no-one is missing. This idea is reinforced in Ezra 6:17 and

23. Grabbe, *Ezra-Nehemiah*, 135.

24. Farisani, "Ezra-Nehemiah," 126.

25. "All Judah" (Neh 13:12); "all the people" (Ezra 3:11; 10:9); in Nehemiah 8 eleven times, and "all the people of Judah and Benjamin" (Ezra 10:9).

8:35 where it is explicitly indicated that the twelve tribes are represented in Judah and Benjamin. Given that this categorization excludes the other ten tribes of Israel and converts them into foreigners, the article concludes that the concept of "all Israel" in Ezra-Nehemiah is used to promote an exclusivist ethnic ideology.

"Enemies" (אִיבִים/צָרִים)

In Ezra, the word used for "adversary" or "enemy" is צַר and in Nehemiah אִיב. Both words basically carry the same sentiment. According to James Swanson, צַר means "enemy, foe, adversary, opponent, i.e., one in a state of open hostility with an opponent."[26] Moreover, according to Koehler and Baumgartner, אִיב means "to be hostile towards".[27] In Ezra 4, "enemies" is described as צָרִים יְהוּדָה וּבִינְיָמִן (enemies of Judah and Benjamin) and in Nehemiah 6 as אוֹיְבֵינוּ (our enemies). The enemies in Ezra 4 are thus men who approached Zerubbabel and the heads of families to offer assistance in building the temple because they also worshipped the same Yahweh that Zerubbabel and others in the community worshipped. In turn, Zerubbabel, Jeshua, and the so-called rest of the heads of the families of Israel made it clear that they are not going to allow them to take part in building the temple. In the manner in which the narrator presents the story, the enmity among these groups is presupposed without prior evidence. It is therefore difficult to view a pledge of solidarity and an intention to contribute towards the building of the temple as an act of enmity, especially if it is because both parties worship the same God. In the same vein, the enmity in Nehemiah 6 is presupposed without prior indications towards open hostility between the parties. Nehemiah reports that after he finished the wall, his so-called enemies invited him to a meeting in one of the villages in the plain of Ono. But, according to him, they intended to do him harm (Neh 6:2). Commenting on the invitations of Nehemiah by Sanballat who was Tobiah's colleague, Lester Grabbe says:

> [T]he invitations to meet, which Nehemiah interpreted as ruses to do him in, could have been genuine efforts to come to some sort of *modus vivendi*. Sanballat might have realized that he had to accept Nehemiah's presence and a move at conciliation could

---

26. Swanson, *Dictionary of Biblical Language*.

27. Koehler and Baumgartner, *Lexicon in Veteris Testamentis*, 35.

be to mutual advantage. Having only Nehemiah's version of events means that evaluating the truth behind his accusations is difficult.[28]

Nehemiah further reports: "Moreover in those days the nobles of Judah sent many letters to Tobiah, and Tobiah's letters came to them" (Neh 6:17). Also, the nobles of Judah spoke of Tobiah's good deeds in Nehemiah's presence, and reported Nehemiah's words to Tobiah. These reports by Nehemiah reveal another side of the situation. The nobles of Judah were friendly to Tobiah. Also in Neh 13:4–8, Nehemiah is at odds with Tobiah and Eliashib, the priest whom Tobiah befriended. Given this state of affairs, one may suppose that Tobiah, and by implication, the so-called enemies, were actually not enemies of the Judeans, but rather that Nehemiah perceived them as enemies.

This essay suggests that one should perceive Nehemiah's behavior in terms of a broader framework. I propose that Nehemiah's behavior was reflective of a particular thought-pattern as outlined well by Joseph Blenkinsopp:

> Nehemiah is presented not only as a member of the upper-class *golah* segment of the population but also as an exponent of the rigorist legalism which characterized Ezra and his associates. This quasisectarian orientation, with its roots in the eastern diaspora and its orientation heavily dependent on Deuteronomistic theology and the teaching of Ezekiel and his school, was a significant factor in Nehemiah's conflictual relations with the lay and especially the priestly aristocracy in the province. His ejection of Tobiah from the temple precincts and ritual purification of the space he had occupied (13:4–9) is one pointer in this direction.[29]

Blenkinsopp's description of Nehemiah "as an exponent of the rigorist legalism which characterized Ezra" is central to Lester Grabbe's argument. According to Grabbe, Nehemiah was indeed a reformer with a program that explains a number of his actions.[30] What eventually emerges is a man obsessed with a particular vision of the province of Yehud and of Judaism in its widest sense. Grabbe continues to argue that the various measures instigated by Nehemiah[31] were not just miscellaneous *ad hoc* decisions,

28. Grabbe, *Ezra-Nehemiah*, 187.

29. Blenkinsopp, *Judaism, the First Phase*, 115.

30. Grabbe, *Ezra-Nehemiah*, 172.

31. Whether the repair of the wall, the opposition to Sanballat and other "foreigners," the ban on mixed marriages, or even the regulations about the Sabbath.

but rather part of a complete program. In that sense, Nehemiah was very much a reformer. It seems that Nehemiah's goal was no less than to make Judah into an isolated puritanical theocratic state. This program is nowhere explicitly laid out in the book, but the whole thrust of the book is towards this goal.[32] Unfortunately, this program kick-started an identity formation process which produced what Lawrence Wills calls an "opposition-creat-ing-identity."[33] Once again, we see that the term "enemy" in Ezra-Nehemiah was used to render service to an exclusivist ethnic ideology.

OTHER IDEOLOGIES IN EZRA–NEHEMIAH

In this essay, I argue that there is an exclusivist ethnic ideology at work in Ezra-Nehemiah. I further argue that the narrator suppresses the views of other characters in the narrative. We do not hear the dissenting voices in that particular community. For example, we know very little about the people of Israel, including the priests and the Levites who did not keep themselves separate from the neighboring peoples (Ezra 9:1); Shemaiah whom Nehemiah suspected of pronouncing the prophecy against him be-cause Tobiah and Sanballat hired him (Neh 6:12); the prophetess Noadiah and the rest of the prophets who wanted to make Nehemiah afraid (Neh 6:14); the nobles of Judah who were friendly to Tobiah (Neh 6:17–19); the priest Eliashib who allowed Tobiah to stay in the temple chamber, as well as others. All of these characters were not afforded an opportunity to justify their actions in the narrative. It may well be that they had differing opinions from the official ideology reflected in Ezra-Nehemiah. From reading other biblical books, one is made aware of other inclusive ethnic ideologies of the Second Temple period, e.g., Trito-Isaiah, Jonah, and Chronicles. Due to practical constraints, I cannot examine all these books, so I will briefly ex-amine Chronicles as an example of a counter-ideology. In terms of Chron-icles, I will examine two ideological aspects which will be used to illustrate the contrast between the dominant and counter-ideologies, i.e., the concept of "all Israel" as well as the attitude towards foreigners in Chronicles.

---

32 Grabbe, *Ezra-Nehemiah*, 172; Grabbe, *A History of the Jews and Judaism*, 307.

33. Wills, *Not God's People*, 59.

"All Israel" (כָּל־יִשְׂרָאֵל) *in Chronicles*

The term "all Israel" (כָּל־יִשְׂרָאֵל) occurs forty-six times in Chronicles and appears in passages transferred verbatim from Samuel-Kings, sometimes with major or minor changes in the Chronicler's own work (his Sondergut).[34] In Chronicles, this concept is used in reference to the united kingdom,[35] the Northern Kingdom,[36] and the Southern Kingdom (2 Chr 12:1, 2 Chr 24:5 and 2 Chr 28:23). It is significant how the twelve-tribe theme remains prominent in all of the different contexts reflected in Chronicles, from the time of David and Solomon until the postexilic period.

In Chronicles, the twelve-tribe theme is presented, on the one hand, as a socio-political reality and, on the other hand, as an ideal that formed the basis of the Chronicler's vision of a restored Israel. In 2 Chr 30:1–12, one sees something of the existence of the twelve tribes even if it appears against the backdrop of a divided kingdom. The twelve-tribe identity is thus maintained long after the Northern kingdom has disappeared (2 Chr 35:18). In 1 Chr 9:2–3, the twelve-tribe identification is evident even though the text is referring to the postexilic community. This continuing emphasis on a twelve-tribe identity in spite of the changing socio-political context is a sign of the strong religious conviction of the Chronicler that envisioned the twelve tribes as a unity, hence explaining the concept of "all Israel" which in Chronicles serves an inclusive ethnic ideology.

The Foreigners (הַנָּכְרִי) *in Chronicles*

Chronicles was written during the postexilic era when the question of the foreigners was central. The Chronicler's portrayal of Huram, the king of Tyre, as acknowledging YHWH as the creator of heaven and earth (2 Chr 2:12), as well as his portrayal of Huram-abi, a skilled Tyrian artisan, as a son of a Danite[37] woman (2 Chr 2:13–14) defy the dominant bias against foreigners that is evident in Ezra-Nehemiah.[38] This counter-ideology evident

---

34. Cezula, "Identity Formation," 173–74.

35. 1 Chr 9:1; 11:10; 12:38[MT 39]; 13:5; 15:3; 28:4, 8; 29:21, 23, 25, 26; 2 Chr 1:2a, 2b; 7:6; 29:24a, 24b; 30:5 and 35:3.

36. 2 Chr 11:13; 13:4, 15; 30:1, 6 and 2 Chr 31:1.

37. Dan is one the twelve tribes of Israel, which makes a Tyrian a relative of Israel.

38. Both these specific portrayals are not found in 1 Kgs 5:7–9, a parallel of 2 Chronicles 2:11–16.

in this positive portrayal of foreigners is intertwined with the construction of the first temple which constitutes a colossal building project in the history of Israel. The persistent positive portrayal of foreign monarchs in Chronicles, for example, King Huram of Tyre (2 Chr 2:12), the Queen of Sheba (2 Chr 9:7–9), King Neco of Egypt (2 Chr 35:20–27), and King Cyrus of Persia (2 Chr 36:23), points to a particular trend within the Chronicler's narrative, i.e., that the Chronicler's theology with regard to foreigners is rooted in a universalistic ideological framework. Commenting on Neco and Cyrus, Louis Jonker states:

> It is clear that the Chronicler, although acknowledging the political and military power of these foreign monarchs, portrays them as being under Yahweh's dominion. These kings are not portrayed as antagonists in history but rather as those characters who are acting out Yahweh's plan in history.[39]

2 Chronicles 6:32 is another text that is helpful in investigating the ideology of the Chronicler with regard to foreigners. In this text, King Solomon is portrayed as pleading for the foreigner so that the foreigner can enter the temple and be granted his/her request. Also, the foreigner is implicitly portrayed by the Chronicler as knowing God in the present.[40] The parallel to this verse in 2 Kgs 8:41–42, on the other hand, points into the future for the foreigners to know God. To know Israel's God is a positive thing. The Chronicler presents God as a universal God; his reign has no boundaries. He rules over Israel and foreigners as well. This sentiment is actually already present from the beginning of Chronicles in the genealogies. In the genealogical introduction, the Chronicler affirms that all human beings originate from the protohuman, Adam. In other words, nations are not only different; they also have a common origin. We thus see in Chronicles how the concept of foreigners is used to promote an inclusive ethnic ideology.

A BIBLICAL PARADIGM FOR A THEOLOGY OF RECONSTRUCTION IN AFRICA?

In examining Ezra-Nehemiah it became clear that Israel consisted of only Judah and Benjamin. The other ten tribes and those Judahites and Benjaminites who were not exiled were no more part of Israel but foreigners and by

---

39. Jonker, "Who Constitutes Society?," 717.

40. Cezula, "Identity Formation," 189–90.

virtue thereof "enemies of Judah." Furthermore, those who were considered traditional foreigners were associated with "abominations" (תּוֹעֵבוֹת) and considered enemies of Judah. Ezra-Nehemiah thus propagated an exclusivist ethnic ideology which produced an "opposition-creating-identity."

In Chronicles, on the other hand, Israel is idealized in terms of the original twelve tribes. The Chronicler held a strong religious conviction that envisioned the twelve tribes as a unity. Additionally, the foreigners were seen as originating from Adam, just like Israel. Despite Israel's election by YHWH, all humanity still falls under his dominion and God uses even the foreigners, who also know about him, to carry out his orders. Chronicles thus propagated an inclusive ethnic ideology with unifying tendencies vis-à-vis Ezra-Nehemiah's divisive tendencies.

However, which of these two biblical ideologies offers the best possibility to serve as a biblical paradigm for a theology of reconstruction in Africa? By de-ideologizing Ezra-Nehemiah, we have identified the prevalent ideology in Ezra-Nehemiah in addition to other competing ideologies of the Second Temple period, specifically the Chronicler's ideology. Since this is not merely a theological exercise but a contribution to a search for a biblical paradigm for a reconstruction theology in Africa as well, it is proper to make some suggestions as to which of these two ideologies has the potential to serve reconstruction in Africa better.

In this essay, we have examined some of the reconstruction processes taking place in Ezra-Nehemiah and Chronicles with the intention of assessing their ideological effects. By means of illustration, we will look at the way in which the construction of the two temples is depicted in the respective texts. We start with the second temple in Ezra-Nehemiah and finish with the first temple in Chronicles.

The Second Temple

The rebuilding of the temple in Ezra-Nehemiah is informed by an exclusivist ethnic ideology. Ezra 4 demonstrates the impact of this ideology on reconstruction quite well. The so-called adversaries and the "people of the land" are excluded from the reconstruction of the temple irrespective of what they can offer but just because of who they are. Despite being Yahwists, the so-called adversaries were rejected. Ezra-Nehemiah thus focused on difference instead of similarity. The rejection of the "people of the land" sets the tone for the rest of the narrative that centered on the reconstruction of the temple. The "people of the land" reacted to their exclusion by engaging in social action which expressed their disapproval of their exclusion. So we see how the "people of the land" resorted to a variety of different strategies:

> Then the people of the land discouraged the people of Judah, and made them afraid to build, and they bribed officials to frustrate their plan throughout the reign of King Cyrus of Persia and until the reign of King Darius of Persia. In the reign of Ahasuerus, in his accession year, they wrote an accusation against the inhabitants of Judah and Jerusalem (Ezra 4:4–6).

> At that time the work on the house of God in Jerusalem stopped and was discontinued until the second year of the reign of King Darius of Persia (Ezra 4:24).

Farisani explains the people's resistance as follows: "the עַם הָאָרֶץ were not merely opposed to the rebuilding of the temple, rather, they were opposed to their exclusion from the rebuilding process."[41] The result of the people's opposition was the stalling of the reconstruction process. The narrator states that the work on the house of the Lord was stopped from the time of Cyrus until the time of Darius (Ezra 4:5), a period of nineteen or twenty years. We thus see that due to an exclusivist ethnic ideology, the reconstruction process was hindered.

The First Temple

During the time of David and Solomon, Israelite worship was being reconstructed from a decentralized system of worship to a centralized one. The temple therefore, was a project of this broader reconstruction process. Of utmost interest for this current discussion is an ideology that informed this reconstruction project, namely, the account depicting the building of the first temple. In 2 Chr 2:11–16, Solomon assembled people who were best qualified because of their skills and not because of who they were. King Solomon invited King Huram who was a foreigner, i.e., a Tyrian. Solomon explains why he requests Huram when he says, "for I know that your servants are skilled in cutting Lebanon timber. My servants will work with your servants" (2 Chr 2:8–9). Solomon's project was thus characterized not

---

41. Farisani, "Ezra-Nehemiah," 127.

by conflict but rather by enhanced solidarity. The results of the approach Solomon adopted are revealed in at least two verses:

> Thus Solomon finished the house of the Lord and the king's house; all that Solomon had planned to do in the house of the Lord and in his own house he successfully accomplished (2 Chr 7:11).

> Thus all the work of Solomon was accomplished from the day the foundation of the house of the Lord was laid until the house of the Lord was finished completely (2 Chr 8:16).

The inclusivist ethnic ideology portrayed by the Chronicler in Solomon facilitated the reconstruction process. This portrayal of the Solomonic temple building by the Chronicler carried some message for the Chronicler's own time. The Chronicler's narrative is not in itself an indication of a historical reality during the time of Solomon. It is rather a construction of the past in order to influence the Chronicler's presence. The Chronicler probably wrote in a time when the Zerubbabel temple was already finished. He could therefore not have influenced the process of temple building by his writings. However, by means of his portrayal of the Solomonic temple, the Chronicler probably wanted to restore the community's evaluation of the Zerubbabel temple in their own time. Because of the controversy around the rebuilding as described in Ezra-Nehemiah, the Second Temple always had a "legitimacy" problem. The Chronicler probably wanted to address this legitimacy problem by showing that it is no problem that foreigners were around during the reconstruction. That was also the case during Solomon's temple building!

The Chronicler also probably wanted to show that an inclusivist way of thinking about the temple could benefit the broader community's participation in temple worship, while an exclusivist stance would always place obstacles in the way of full acceptance of the sanctuary. It is important to note that Solomon took seven years to build his temple (1 Kgs 6:38) whereas the exiles took approximately nineteen or twenty years to rebuild it (Ezra 3:8 and 6:15). Lundquist comments as follows on the approximate twelve or thirteen year difference between the durations of the two reconstruction projects:

> That phase of Solomon's temple that was rebuilt by the Jewish people returning from Babylonian Exile (known as the Second

Temple) was much less grand than the original had been, due to the poverty of the people (Hag 2:1–3).[42]

While the members of the postexilic community had fewer resources, their discriminatory attitude blocked them from accepting assistance. The exclusivist ethnic ideology of the exiles delayed the reconstruction of the temple in addition to precipitating social conflict which is not conducive for reconstruction.

In view of this, one could thus argue that Ezra-Nehemiah's exclusivist ideology is not recommendable for reconstruction in (South) Africa, and I would hesitate to recommend Nehemiah as a biblical paradigm for reconstruction theology in (South) Africa. In light of the counter-ideology identified above, it may be that Chronicles is a better candidate for a biblical paradigm for a theology of reconstruction in (South) Africa.

CONCLUSION

The temple constructions as reconstruction projects in both corpora have been examined along with identity processes informing them to assess their ideological effects on reconstruction. It is paramount, however, to first highlight that the idea of reconstruction as perceived in this discussion encapsulates the related notions of renewal, redress, reform, transformation, and reconciliation. Social relations therefore become a central concern for a theology of reconstruction in this essay. This is based on the presupposition that exclusivist identity formations are likely to result in social conflict and thereby hinder reconstruction. Inclusivist identity formations, on the other hand, may promote community solidarity and consequently also facilitate reconstruction. We have seen these two positions illustrated well in the respective temple constructions of Ezra-Nehemiah and Chronicles. I therefore advocate a theology of reconstruction that takes cognizance of identity processes and their effects on the process of reconstruction.

One sees the value of such an inclusivist understanding of a theology of reconstruction in two instances in South Africa today, namely, competition for resources and power mongering.

First, competition for resources is a legitimate and a crucial factor for reconstruction. It needs to be managed cautiously to avoid infiltration by exclusivist identity processes that can eventually lead to social conflict at

---

42. Lundquist, "Temple," 1283.

the expense of a reconstruction process that may lead to progress and prosperity. It is likely that the political elite may view their mandate to spearhead reconstruction as authorization to dominate the competition. One such exclusivist identity process concerns ethnic discrimination. Ethnic discrimination can be as devastating as the 1972 and 1993 genocides in Burundi and the 1994 genocide of Rwanda have demonstrated.[43] In some instances, such discriminatory tendencies operate along political party lines. A social border is drawn between the members of the ruling party and the rest of the nation where only members of the ruling party have access to resources. Such identity processes may lead to social conflict and impact badly on reconstruction, and thus ought to be avoided. One particularly harmful identity process in South Africa today that needs to be guarded against is the development of an identity group called tenderpreneurs.[44] "Tenderpreneurship" is an exclusivist identity process that deliberately and unjustly denies out-group social categories the right to fairly compete in the economy. In the long run, it will lead to social conflict which is not conducive for reconstruction.

The second instance in which an inclusivist theology of reconstruction may be helpful is the tendency in South Africa today of power mongering. Power, i.e., the ability to influence other people's behavior, can be earned legitimately through one's position and influence. This is a legitimate form of power which I would characterize as "authority." However, when that ability to have power is used to forcefully persuade people to do things, and is accompanied by a frantic clinging to that power, I would describe it as "power mongering." Power mongering usually breeds exclusivist identity processes that eventually may lead to social conflict. It is indeed unfortunate when leaders perceive reconstruction as a means to nurture their position of power. Usually, power mongers draw social borders between those who are their puppets and those who think independently. The followers of power mongers would then benefit from reconstruction projects while independent thinkers are marginalized. Such a position is an identity process that excludes even party members on grounds of being "too independent" in thinking. Power mongering has a high potential for social

43. According to Femke Eekhof, in Burundi, one finds two different genocides. In 1972 it was the Tutsis killing the Hutus and in 1993 it was *vice versa*—Hutus killing Tutsis. And in neighboring Rwanda, one finds in 1994 Hutus killing Tutsis, "The Great Lakes Region's Genocides," 14–20.

44. These are government officials or politicians who abuse their powers and influence to secure government tenders and contracts.

conflict, tearing apart the community, and as a result is quite negative for reconstruction.

As indicated above, this essay advocates a theology of reconstruction that takes cognizance of identity processes and their effect on reconstruction. The discussion has demonstrated that in Ezra-Nehemiah we find exclusivist identity processes resulting in social conflict and thereby hindering reconstruction. The two examples of competition for resources and power mongering cited above demonstrated that exclusivist identity processes are not conducive to reconstruction. On the other hand, in 2 Chr 2:11–16, we see how a reconstruction project informed by an inclusivist identity process played a positive role in the facilitation of reconstruction. For this reason, it may well be that Chronicles may be a better biblical paradigm for a theology of reconstruction in Africa.

BIBLIOGRAPHY

Blenkinsopp, Joseph. *Judaism, The First Phase: The Place of Ezra and Nehemiah in the Origins of Judaism*. Grand Rapids: Eerdmans, 2009.

Cezula, Ntozakhe S. "Identity Formation and Community Solidarity: Second Temple Historiographies in Discourse with (South) African Theologies of Reconstruction." PhD. diss., Stellenbosch University, 2013.

Eekhof, Femke. "The Great Lakes Region's Genocides: Rwanda and Burundi." No pages. Online: https://openaccess.leidenuniv.nl/handle/1887/19365.

Farisani, Elelwani B. "The Use of Ezra-Nehemiah in a Quest for a Theology of Renewal, Transformation and Reconstruction in the (South) African Context." PhD. diss., University of KwaZulu-Natal, 2002.

Grabbe, Leslie L. *Ezra-Nehemiah*. London: Routledge, 1998.

———. *A History of the Jews and Judaism in the Second Temple Period, Vol. 1. Yehud: A History of the Persian Province of Judah*. London: T. & T. Clark, 2004.

Groenewald, Evert P. "Apartheid en Voogdyskap in die Lig van die Heilige Skrif." In *Regverdige Rasse-Apartheid, edited by Geoffrey Cronjé*, 40–67. Stellenbosch: CSV, 1947.

Hanson, Paul. *The Dawn of Apocalyptic*. Philadelphia: Fortress, 1979.

Jonker, Louis C. *1 & 2 Chronicles*. Understanding the Bible Commentary Series. Grand Rapids: Baker, 2013.

———. "Who Constitutes Society? Yehud's Self-understanding in the Late Persian Era as Reflected in the Books of Chronicle." *Journal of Biblical Literature* 127/4 (2008) 703–24.

Koehler, Ludwig, and Walter Baumgartner. *Lexicon in Veteris Testamenti Libros*. Leiden: Brill, 1958.

Loubser, Johannes A. *The Apartheid Bible: A Critical Review of Racial Theology in South Africa*. Cape Town: Maskew Miller Longman, 1987.

Lundquist, John M. "Temple." In *Eerdmans Dictionary of the Bible*, edited by D. N. Freedman, 1280–84. Grand Rapids: Eerdmans, 2000.

Mugambi, Jesse N. K. *Christian Theology and Social Reconstruction*. Nairobi: Acton, 2003.

Nuremberg Trial Proceedings, Volume 12. "One Hundred and Eleventh Day to the One Hundred and Nineteenth Day". Online: http://www.loc.gov/rr/frd/Military_Law/pdf/NT_Vol-XII.pdf

Sharp, Carolyn J. *Prophecy and Ideology in Jeremiah: Struggles for Authority in the Deutero-Jeremianic Prose*. London: T. & T. Clark, 2003.

Smith-Christopher, Daniel L. "Exile." In *Eerdmans Dictionary of the Bible*, edited by D. N. Freedman, 439–40. Grand Rapids: Eerdmans, 2000.

Swanson, James. *A Dictionary of Biblical Languages with Semantic Domains: Hebrew (Old Testament)*. Oak Harbor, WA: Logos Research Systems, 1997.

Tatum, Lynn. "People of the Land." In *Eerdmans Dictionary of the Bible*, edited by D. N. Freedman, 1027. Grand Rapids: Eerdmans, 2000.

Weanzana, Nupanga. "Ezra." In *Africa Bible Commentary*, edited by T. Adeyemo, 531–42. Nairobi: World Alive, 2006.

Wills, Lawrence M. *Not God's People: Insiders and Outsiders in the Biblical World*. Lanham: Rowman & Littlefield Publishers, 2008.

Yee, Gale A. "The Author/Text/Reader and Power: Suggestions for a Critical Framework for Biblical Studies." In *Reading from this Place, Volume 1: Social Location and Biblical Interpretation in the United States*, edited by Fernando F. Segovia and Mary Ann Tolbert, 109–18. Minneapolis: Fortress, 1995.

PART 5

Responses

8

Dignity for All:
Humanity in the
Context of Creation

Jacqueline E. Lapsley,
Princeton Theological Seminary

THE WHOLE CANON OF Scripture forms us, forms the character of our communities, is the crux of meaningful Old Testament reflection. This idea,
articulated by Bruce Birch at the beginning of this sparkling collection
of essays on human dignity, has been very much alive, if not universally
embraced, for some time among Old Testament ethicists. Despite widespread agreement and discussion, this idea of ethical formation as canonical formation has not made its way more substantively into Christian
communities, likely due to the difficulty of articulating exactly what such
formation looks like.

The essays in this volume attest to the truth of Birch's claim that narrative is of primary significance in ethical interpretation of the Bible—almost
all the essays take up biblical narrative(s) as their way into thinking with
the Bible about human dignity. One could surely consider human dignity

through the lens of law or wisdom, but it is not by chance that so many authors in this volume interpret stories: as Martha Nussbaum and others have shown, stories tell us who we are and how we should live.[1]

In this brief response, I will not be able to attend to all of these excellent essays individually. Instead, I will touch on several, and then observe some themes running through the collection.

Human dignity is, as so many of these essays underscore, critical to affirm in an era when it is under such acute threat around the world. Certainly this emphasis on human dignity has been in continuity with the traditional emphasis in the Christian tradition on the central role of humanity within creation, on the *imago dei* as a core theological doctrine. Yet, as Patricia Tull in her recent book, *Inhabiting Eden*,[2] among others has shown, such an emphasis without a clear understanding of humanity within the context of the rest of creation is destructive for nonhuman creation. Furthermore, human dignity itself is diminished and distorted from its true form unless humanity is situated within its interdependent relationships with the rest of creation. Bruce Birch gets at this affirmation in his essay by focusing on the dignity of human beings within the context of creation in the Old Testament. Human dignity can only be understood within a context of creational dignity.

In her essay on violence and human dignity, Juliana Claassens turns our attention to Rizpah, whose mourning over the dead for six months stands as a powerful witness against the violence raging around her. Rizpah's testimony is reminiscent of Leymah Gbowee, whose organizing of women in Liberia formed a powerful and effective nonviolent testimony against the violence plaguing that country in the 2000s. In both cases women manifest the "common vulnerability" in ways that testify to human dignity and potentially activate political and social change. Claassens' discussion also stimulates us to consider what a lack of mourning means in the current U.S. context of an addiction to endless war. How might this "weapon of the weak" be effective when there are no interludes to war anymore, when violence is both unceasing and normalized?

In his reading of Judges 19–21, Douglas Lawrie hits the mark when he attributes the rhetorical shaping of the narrative to the author's subtlety in seeing the atrocities against women depicted as "an index of social decadence." I would only add that the social decadence is the direct result of

1. Nussbaum, *Love's Knowledge*.
2. Tull, *Inhabiting Eden*.

this nadir in Israel's relationship with YHWH, thus the social situation is the consequence of Israel's failure to attend to their life with God. The last chapters of Judges provide a nightmarish portrait of an anthropocentric universe. As Lawrie notes: "The abomination makes [the author's] point." Lawrie's imaginative exercise of conversing with the author of Judges 19–21 serves as a helpful caution against ferociously judgmental scholarly critiques that fail to understand the reading encounter as a face-to-face one. Lawrie does not invoke Levinas,[3] but he might have. Lawrie's larger point, that our judgments of others reenact the dehumanizing acts they have committed, is insightful. "In the interest of human dignity, we have to award [perpetrators] faces, not categorize them under ideological rubrics, speak to and of their unique dignity, not deny their humanity." This does not mean endorsing abominable acts; it means engaging human beings as such. The connection between dignity and an appropriate sense of nontoxic shame that Lawrie asserts is one that gets lost in much contemporary discourse, scholarly and otherwise.

One theme, discernible in several essays in one way or another (Gerald West, Ntozakhe Cezula, Douglas Lawrie) concerns the ambiguity of the Bible. The Bible itself acknowledges the problem; after all, Satan tempts Jesus in the wilderness by interpreting Scripture. Douglas Lawrie suggests that the Bible, like fire, is both "useful and dangerous," so the pressing question is how to read it so that it is "useful," that is, with human dignity as central focus. Augustine famously asserted that, "the fulfillment and end of Scripture is the love of God and our neighbor." It might behoove us to clarify Augustine: "the fulfillment and end of scripture is the love of God and *the dignity* of our neighbor." The list of historical efforts to "love" the neighbor that are, at root, exercises in patronizing condescension, stretches to the heavens. A focus on human dignity within the context of creational dignity is a more robust hermeneutic; it is a stronger bulwark against all the "love" that in reality masks self-love.

Several of the essays, whether implicitly or explicitly, invoke James Scott's "hidden transcript" as a means of articulating human dignity among marginalized populations.[4] The idea of the "hidden transcript" has been a rich resource in scholarly discourse (though sometimes critiqued and/or modified) for thinking about the ways in which ancient communities engaged dominant cultures (especially in the way apocalyptic developed).

3. Levinas, *Totality and Infinity*.
4. Scott, *Domination and the Arts of Resistance*.

These essays reveal it to be an equally powerful resource for interpreting the Bible with a view toward upholding and enacting the human dignity of marginalized persons and communities today.

BIBLIOGRAPHY

Levinas, Emmanuel. *Totality and Infinity: An Essay on Exteriority.* Pittsburgh, PA: Duquesne University Press, 1969.

Nussbaum, Martha. *Love's Knowledge: Essays on Philosophy and Literature.* New York: Oxford University Press, 1990.

Scott, James C. *Domination and the Arts of Resistance: Hidden Transcripts.* New Haven, CT: Yale University Press, 1990.

Tull, Patricia K. *Inhabiting Eden: Christians, the Bible, and the Ecological Crisis.* Louisville, KY: Westminster John Knox, 2013.

9

Human Rights, Human Dignity, and the HIV/AIDS Pandemic

Cheryl B. Anderson,
Garrett-Evangelical Theological Seminary

THE CONCEPTS OF "HUMAN rights" and "human dignity" are inextricably related. The preamble of the United Nations Declaration of Human Rights begins with the assertion that the "recognition of the inherent dignity and of the equal and inalienable rights of all members of the human family is the foundation of freedom, justice and peace in the world."[1] Essentially, human dignity is the basis from which human rights flow and, without according human beings their basic rights, sustainable "freedom, justice and peace" cannot be attained.

Although we could agree in theory that all human beings should be treated with dignity and have rights, we know that, in practice, some human beings are treated differently. Some of those who are not deemed to have equal dignity or rights are women, LGBTQ persons, and those who are different by reason of race, ethnicity, or religion. Unfortunately, such

---

1. http://www.un.org/en/documents/udhr/.

discriminatory practices are often justified on the basis of a faith tradition, such as Christianity, and its sacred text, the Bible. As a result, the Bible is read in ways that support the subordination of women, the condemnation of homosexuality, and the exclusion of those who are of different races, ethnic groups, and religions.

The articles in this volume, as organized under three headings, identify the harm caused by such exclusionary and discriminatory biblical readings: violence against women and the queer community, systemic injustice, and xenophobic anxieties. In response, each of these articles offers a biblical reading that could help to counter the harmful effects of such traditional biblical understandings. Consequently, there is a pattern in this volume: a problem is identified in the heading and the articles under the heading offer an alternative biblical reading that could help to improve the identified problem. Yet these articles actually do more. As I read these articles, I found guidance on how a problem that is not even mentioned in the headings could be countered: the HIV/AIDS pandemic. For example, the Bible has been read to blame those who are HIV-positive for their status. They are told that they are positive because God has punished them because of their sins, thus contributing to the stigma and discrimination that they experience, and making it less likely that others in the community will get tested or, if necessary, begin treatment. Biblical scholars in South Africa have offered closer readings of texts that counter that notion of God's punishment, and these readings help to remove stigma and, in turn, restore human dignity.[2]

Furthermore, scholar/activist colleagues in Southern Africa have taught me that the AIDS pandemic is primarily a social justice problem.[3] The specific social justice issue is the economic, social, and cultural marginalization of certain groups: women, the poor, LGBTQ persons and, as has become increasingly clear from the statistics on new infections, black people on both sides of the Atlantic Ocean. Such marginalization—involving such dynamics as unequal pay, fewer educational opportunities, and limited access to needed resources—is problematic because it is the setting in which HIV thrives. If we are to prevent new infections, then, we must stop marginalizing groups of people. Since marginalization correspondingly undermines the human dignity of affected groups, the Bible must be read in ways that end marginalization and thereby restore human dignity.

2. West, "Reading Job positively"; Nadar, "Barak God and Die!"

3. Dube, *The HIV & AIDS Bible*; Phiri, et al., *African Women*.

To me, these articles offer three significant ways that the human dignity of marginalized groups can be restored.

First, Bruce Birch reminds us that the exodus event is set in motion by the people of God who cry out because of their harsh conditions. They are not even crying out to God specifically, they are just crying out because of their misery—and God hears them (Exod 3:7–8a). As Birch notes, "human moral concern cannot passively wait for the activity of God, but is called to be fully engaged in God's moral concern and action." It is therefore incumbent upon those communities that suffer disproportionately from HIV and AIDS to cry out because that act can set God's saving activity in motion. Similarly, Juliana Claassens' reading of 2 Samuel 21:1–14 shows that Rizpah's mourning moved a privileged individual—a king—to act compassionately. From these two articles, crying out and mourning are forms of resistance, a protest against harsh conditions, that can prompt both human and divine responses.

Second, Charlene van der Walt's reading of Genesis 38 shows us how Tamar's deceiving of Judah was a way that someone without power can "unmask the injustice committed by the perpetrator." In addition, such encounters force the one with power to recognize the humanity of the one who had previously been "other." As a result, those who are marginalized can resist dehumanization and become active agents in the transformation of unjust relationships.[4] Resisting dehumanization, then, becomes a strategy to resist marginalization and those corresponding conditions that contribute to higher HIV infection rates.

Finally, Gerald West points out the similarities between the economic inequities of the apartheid system and those of a postapartheid globalized capitalism. Similarly, Van der Walt mentions that references to cultural traditions that justify the subordination of women or the condemnation of homosexuality tend to forget the diversity of African traditions and the plurality of human experiences. To me, such discussions indicate that African communities, whether on the continent or in the diaspora, must recognize the ways in which we have been marginalized—as well as the ways in which we marginalize some of those within our own communities. Therefore, we must fight against marginalization that undermines human dignity, whether it begins outside or inside of our communities, if we are to end the HIV/AIDS pandemic.

4. Claassens, "Resisting Dehumanization."

In summary, the articles in this volume offer some helpful guidance on restoring human dignity and eliminating marginalization. During recent visits to Brazil and Cuba, I was reminded of the importance of human rights (and the related concept of human dignity) to combat the spread of HIV. Both countries have a strong national commitment to human rights and the right to health care which have resulted in HIV infection rates that are consistently lower than those in South Africa or the United States.

In spite of affirming the need for restorative readings, these same articles recognize that transformation will be difficult because churches in specific contexts can be disconnected from the socio-economic realities around them (cf. West, in this volume) and the Bible itself contains ideologies that promote marginalization (cf. Cezula, in this volume). In addition, Christians are taught to be suspicious of "human rights" because they are viewed as secular and not biblical. But such rights are based on the inherent dignity of all human beings, as created in the image of God (Gen 1:27), and true freedom, justice and peace—shalom—will not occur until those rights are recognized. On that day, marginalization will be eliminated, human dignity will be restored, and the inequities that fuel new HIV infections will be erased.

BIBLIOGRAPHY

Claassens, L. Juliana. "Resisting Dehumanization: Ruth, Tamar, and the Quest for Human Dignity." *Catholic Biblical Quarterly* 74/4 (2012) 659–74.

Dube, Musa W. *The HIV & AIDS Bible: Selected Essays.* Scranton: University of Scranton Press, 2008.

Nadar, Sarojini. "'*Barak* God and Die!': Women, HIV, and AIDS and a Theology of Suffering." In *Grant Me Justice!: HIV/AIDS & Gender Readings of the Bible*, edited by Musa W. Dube and Musimbi R. Kanyoro, 60–79. Maryknoll, NY: Orbis, 2004.

Phiri, Isabel Apawo, Beverley Haddad, and Madipoane Masenya. *African Women, HIV/AIDS and Faith Communities.* Pietermaritzburg: Cluster, 2003.

West, Gerald. "Reading Job 'positively' in the context of HIV and AIDS in South Africa." *Concilium* 4 (2004) 112–24.

10

In Conversation:
The Old Testament, Ethics, and Human Dignity

Dion Forster,
Faculty of Theology, Stellenbosch University

CONVERSATION AND ETHICS

CONVERSATION IS AN IMMENSELY powerful aspect of what it means to be human. In a good conversation you transcend the limit of the "self" and you are enabled to experience something of the "other." As the "other" person speaks you begin to hear and even understand, to some extent, something of who they are and their perspective on reality. When it is your turn to speak, you also seek to express your conviction and understanding of the world for the listener to engage and consider. Levinas posits that the engagement between the self and the other frames not only our view of the world, but our very identity.[1] He regards it as the basis for ethics. In short, conversation is critical to ethics.

1. Robbins, *Is It Righteous to Be?*, 105–6.

ETHICS AND HOSPITALITY

Good conversation requires hospitality:[2] a space in which the "self" and the "other" can give safe and full expression of their points of view, knowing that what they share will be held with care and considered with honest and open respect. It does not presuppose full agreement. To be hospitable to the "other" always requires some measure of self-sacrifice. For example, when we welcome a stranger into our home our regular rhythms are disrupted, our own preferences and needs are placed in a counterbalance with the preferences and needs of our guest. We may even need to unlearn some things such as habits, and learn some new things, such as a new vocabulary.[3] If, however, we have the courage and grace to create this space for conversation, there is a possibility that something beautiful may take place: the forging of a new friendship; the discovery of shared interests; perhaps even the gift of new ways of relating to the world through the life of the "other."[4] In short, such engagement changes not only what we do, but who we are. Bruce Birch rightly says that this is the essence of Christian ethics; it is "not simply concerned with moral conduct but also with moral character."

The work of Christian ethics is the work of careful conversation about what we do and who we are. The ethicist seeks to facilitate open and honest conversations between persons, beliefs, ideas, texts, and social concerns with an outcome in mind. The desired outcome of such conversation is to be able to understand and to give expression to what we believe to be the most true, just, and desirable reality and how we should live in order to foster this reality. This may include elements such as obedience to God's will, honoring the dignity of all human persons, and being faithful stewards of the earth.

---

2. Vosloo, *Engele as gaste?*, 47, 129, 135.

3. In the last five years I have traveled to well over one hundred countries. I am always fascinated and amazed by cultural and linguistic differences among the people that I visit which include elements such as the structure of the day, how and where food is eaten, and where family and friends meet one another. I am also always struck by how differently our vocabulary is formed. In South African English a "robot" is a traffic light; of course the word "robot" refers to something quite different in the English of the UK and the USA.

4. For a wonderful example of this, see Stanley Hauerwas' chapter on the importance of conversation and friendship in Stanley Hauerwas, *Working with Words*, especially 272–74.

PLACE AND PEOPLE

This present volume is a wonderful example of just such a conversation. It is a conversation between the Old Testament, ethics, and human dignity. Bruce Birch helps us to understand two critical aspects of this conversation, namely, the place and the people. The place, or space, within which the conversation takes place is the biblical text; the Old Testament in particular. Next, Birch introduces us to the four conversation partners, namely, the Old Testament, ethics, human dignity, and you, the reader. As I read the book, I found that a conversation in this space, with these participants, deeply challenged my perspectives on the Old Testament in relation to ethics and human dignity.

LANGUAGE AND INTENTION

Our location gives us a common language—the Old Testament text. In this case, the common language is not only the text itself, but more importantly the intention of the canon of the Old Testament. Birch rightly points out that on issues of ethics and human dignity, such as those discussed in this book, Christians have often turned to the Bible for moral guidance. We tend to ask a primary question of the Bible: "What shall we do?"

Most often, this is not a conversation that seeks to understand the world and will of the "other"—in this case the biblical text. Rather, it is simply seen as needing to find two or three verses, or a biblical worldview, that give authority to our already-held beliefs and desired intentions. It disregards the reality that before the words and ideas of the books of the Old Testament were written, before they were put together in the canon, they emerged within a particular context with social, ethical, and religious concerns. The context in which they emerged matters—it is the context of the "other." We need to create space for it and not simply collapse it into our own.

This being said, Birch points out, with reference to the work of Eckart Otto,[5] that the Old Testament does have clear moral texts, and that ethics in the Old Testament should not merely be relegated to a historical and theological study of the Israelite religion. The mistake that we often make is trying to make a direct application of Old Testament moral texts which are very closely tied to the ancient social contexts of Israel to our contemporary

5. Otto, *Theologische Ethik des Alten Testaments*.

situation, without any translation. We make the mistake of thinking that the "other" is as we are and so expresses reality in exactly the same way that we do. That is not conversation; it is assimilation without the opportunity for discovery and growth. In a very real sense it is unethical; it denies the dignity of the "other" as a conversation partner.

If we are going to learn anything of value, truths that will shape us for better living, we shall have to be hospitable enough to engage the world, concerns, aspirations, beliefs, and language of the "other." Douglas Lawrie does this masterfully in his chapter *Outrageous Terror and Trying Texts*. Rather than dismissing difficult texts, or disregarding them, he facilitates a rich and textured conversation in a common language—the language of the aspiration and intent of the Old Testament. In encountering the "other," we unmask something in ourselves: "We may be overtaken, not by the awareness of our no doubt laudable motives and our no doubt ineluctable contexts, but by the negative self-awareness that we could have read and judged differently."

OLD TESTAMENT ETHICS AND MORAL FORMATION

Ntozakhe Cezula also facilitates such a hospitable conversation in his chapter *De-Ideologizing Ezra-Nehemiah*. It is precisely in understanding the exclusive identity processes at play in Ezra-Nehemiah (the conversation partner) that he is able to ask deeper questions; not just, "what shall we do?" but more importantly, "who shall we be?"

The question of moral character was of central concern to the writers of the Old Testament (see Birch's discussion). In their attempt to live as moral beings, expressed both in moral conduct and moral character, they engaged the reality of their context. What emerged from that is the variety of moral perspectives we discover in the Old Testament. An open, honest, hospitable conversation with the text shapes both who we are and what we shall do. The engagement with the "other" of the text opens up our own world so that we can discover who we should be. Juliana Claassens' chapter on Rizpah's lament in 2 Sam 21:1–14 is a good example of this. She says the following:

> This narrative as told in 2 Samuel 21 opens up space for the reader to make sense of other traumatic experiences—the dialogical exchange with other situations of trauma making it possible to

recognize connections between other individuals and groups suffering violence.

While we recognize that many of the problems we face as Christians stem from the Bible itself (take, for example, the well-known issue of heteronormativity that also is treated in Van der Walt's chapter *Reading Queer Lies to Reveal Straight Truth in Genesis 38*), we can also find great moral and ethical value in a careful engagement with the text. Christians claim the Bible as an authoritative text for our faith and life.[6] It cannot be discarded; it should not be misused; rather, we require a restoration of careful and honest engagement with the biblical text for Christian ethics.

Restorative readings of the Old Testament text are in themselves acts of dignity; they are ethical acts. They take the "other" of the text seriously, carefully seeking to engage the world of the biblical writers with honesty, respect, and care. In this process, the reader discovers some truths about the self and the other that allow for the shaping of both moral action and moral character. This was my experience in reading this volume. Through an encounter with the text my own values and views were challenged, informed, and reshaped. Indeed, my appreciation of the Old Testament as a source of moral behavior and moral character was restored.

BIBLIOGRAPHY

Hauerwas, Stanley. *Working with Words: On Learning to Speak Christian*. Eugene, OR: Cascade, 2011.

Lovin, Robin W. *An Introduction to Christian Ethics: Goals, Duties, and Virtues*. Nashville, TN: Abingdon, 2011.

Otto, Eckart. *Theologische Ethik des Alten Testaments*. Stuttgart: Kohlhammer, 1994.

Robbins, Jill. *Is It Righteous to Be? Interviews with Emmanuel Levinas*. Stanford, CA: Stanford University Press, 2002.

Vosloo, Robert. *Engele as gaste? In gesprek oor gasvryheid teenoor "die ander."* Wellington, South Africa: Lux Verbi, 2006.

6. Lovin, *An Introduction to Christian Ethics*, 167–69.

www.ingramcontent.com/pod-product-compliance
Lightning Source LLC
Chambersburg PA
CBHW061740270326
41928CB00011B/2309